Son

of

A

Bishop

ED Long, Jr.

ED Long, Jr.

ISBN-13: 978-1-7366869-0-4

Son of A Bishop

Contact Information

Email: **Ask@EDLongJr.com**

Website: **www.EDLongJr.com**

Bookings: **Bookings@LongCorporations.com**

Facebook: @EDwardLong

Instagram: @EDLongJnr

TikTok: @EDLongJnr

Twitter: @EDLongJnr

Mailing Address:

2260 Fairburn RD SW #310353, Atlanta, Georgia 30331

3

Preface

Have you ever wondered what it's like to be a preacher's kid?

Are you needing help developing your personality while being under the umbrella of influential parents?

Are your parents leading or serving in a ministry?

Do you need help navigating the nuances of balancing your personal growth and development with the calling or pressures of ministry?

Are you pastoring or leading a ministry while parenting?

Are you struggling to relate to your son or daughter?

Are you looking for insight on how to help your children live a "normal life" while ensuring that they are developing a personal relationship with Jesus Christ and identifying their calling?

"He (ED) is getting into what it's all about being the son of a bishop. I was a son of a bishop, so I know the privileges, but I also knew the pressure. You need this book. It is going to bless you. Many of you are in leadership. You need this for yourself; you need this for your children so that they will be able to relate as son or daughter of leadership.
- Bishop Paul S. Morton, Sr.

I once heard someone say that parenting doesn't come with a manual. I'd like to go a step further and say that neither does being an offspring. Many people viewed Bishop Eddie Lee Long as father, mentor, and coach, yet they weren't residents of his household and couldn't learn many of the lessons that my siblings and I were afforded. The purpose of this book is to highlight how my dad's impact supersedes his transition while empowering parents to be transparent, recover from mistakes, and glean from experiences. This book will also challenge offspring to respect their parents in their humanity, learn from our experiences, and provide insight on personal development while carrying their familial torch.

This book is a collection of 14 stories about my dad and me throughout my life, which will make you laugh, cry, scratch your head, and maybe even say, "hmmm, okay now." Some stories may even ruffle your feathers and cause you to look at either one of us with a side-eye, but trust me, IT'S ALL GOOD...ALL THINGS work together for the good of them that love the Lord, and we love the Lord. Prayerfully by the end of reading this book, many questions you may have had will be answered. The last book my father released before he transitioned is entitled *The Untold Story*. If you haven't read it, I challenge you to read it before continuing to read this one. I view much of this book as the sequel to his. At the end of each chapter, I'll invite you to compare and contrast the characters in my life's stories with those in yours.

The Word of the Lord is a collection of stories from people who were like us to be used by emerging generations to enhance the quality of relationships with one another and God. I recall when my dad received the revelation that the Word of God is simply a story of God the Father and Humanity the Son. I pray that you receive this collection of stories between a father and son as a new testament of sorts.

I watched many people have conditional love for my father, based upon what he could do for them, how he could help them, how he was viewed, and the likes. Many were around when things were good, but some of those same people were nowhere to be found when he was down. I can speak in transparency and truth because my love for my father was never conditional. To abandon him would be to abandon me, to hate him would be to hate myself, to disrespect him would be to disrespect myself. For Jesus said, when you've seen the son, you've seen the father.

As I share my truth, I ask that you read these memoirs with an open mind and spirit. It is the truth that sets us free. Completing this manuscript was liberating, but I couldn't begin this journey until I arrived at a good place internally. I did not want to write from a disposition of disgruntlement, disappointment, anger, sadness, or any other unpleasant sentiment. I wanted to be able to share from a pure place of celebration, having overcome and received greater revelation for the edification of the body of Christ, for the reader, and to tell a greater story.

If we were in seminary, I would challenge you to examine the stories hermeneutically and exegete the stories. This means to allow the Holy Spirit to reveal to you where the characters may have been coming from in their expressions or what may have been going on before each situation, which may have caused them to do, feel and say certain things.

We should position ourselves to be less judgmental and be more compassionate toward one another. Not only will that allow you to extend grace towards my father, others, and I within these stories, but it should challenge you to extend the same grace to those in your own lives. Allow the reflection questions at the end of each chapter to give you things to personally consider. Taking this new testament and directly applying it to your relationships will confirm that I have done my job. God bless you. Don't stop! Keep going!

ED Long, Jr.

Table of Contents

Contact Information 3

Preface.. 4

Acknowledgements.. 10

Introduction 14

Homecoming.. 18

Secure the Bag 35

SexED... 44

Houston, We Have a Problem! 54

Boom!... 64

More with Les 75

Parental Advisory... 90

What Kind of Son Are You?............................... 99

Young Dirty Bishop... 102

The Burden of the Building............................... 125

People Are People 151

One More Rep 168

The Call.. 175

Who's Your Daddy? 193

Outro 228

Legacy Building: Look Book.............................. 231

Acknowledgements

I dedicate this book to my family and relatives; My father, who I believe is the greatest person that I have ever met and whom I attribute much of who I am to his teachings, transparency, work ethic, and his kingdom principles. I miss you dearly and think about you every day. I do not like that God chose to call you home early, but when I think about it, what else was there left for you to do? You had done everything that anyone could ever dream of doing, so you truly died empty. The dash in between your birth and death matters. Your impact was immeasurable. Your legacy continues. They say a good man leaves an inheritance to his children's children. We've inherited so many intangibles from you, and what we haven't received, by faithful works, we soon will. We will ensure that everything left from your kingdom makes it to the third and fourth generation so that the word will remain true of you being a good man.

To my mother, the strongest lady that I know, life dealt you a tough hand, and I'm standing in awe of the fact that you're still in the game and finding ways to win. You did your absolute best in raising me and for that, thank you will never be enough. You are an very attractive lady and I have met many of the men who have told me how they tried to date you before I was born. I'm so glad that you did not pick them and but instead chose my father. That is one of the best choices you made, and I'll always be glad about it.

To my immediate family, relatives, bonus mothers and siblings, collectively we form a blended family. Pop biologically, legally and foster fathered five children: Eric Gagliardi, Jeremy Gunter, Jared Long, Taylor Long, and myself. I am blessed to have four mothers: my biological mother, Vanessa (my bonus mother by marriage, who I affectionately refer to as ML); Marie (my older siblings' biological mother); and Yolunda (my sister's biological mother). Pop preached that the Kingdom of God should be inclusive of people from all races and gender. As his family, we represent the Kingdom of God composed of many children of different races, backgrounds, and nationalities, yet we have one father that loves us all. Thank you for the highs, memories, and challenges in us growing together that have helped me become who I am.

To my friends Joseph and Monte, I'm grateful for your unconditional love, support, and covering. Both of you are my unsung heroes.

To New Birth Missionary Baptist Church, I thank you for helping raise me. Since I was nearly five years old, I have called you home since coming there in 1987. In my travels, I always share with others that the people of New Birth, meaning the congregation, are the most encouraging, loyal, and faithful congregation of people that I have ever encountered. My family is my blood family. New Birth is also my blood family, my blood of the Messiah family. I pray this book helps to bring clarity to various things concerning my life. To my New Birth sister, Deborah Parham, thank you for working on this project with me. You produced an environment for me to be free to fully express myself without restriction. We laughed, we cried, we encouraged each other, and we GOT IT DONE!

To Dr. CeCe Covington, thank you for your diligence and perseverance, literally burning the midnight oil, to ensure that this work was edited, formatted, and prepared for print. I'm truly thankful for the lessons learned and the relationship that we've formed.

To Purple Haze, I am thankful for the fruit of your womb and for your nurturing love. God has used you to supply motherly love in a time that I most needed it.

To Laidy, thank you for loving me in the unique ways that only you could. I'm happy to call you home and I am very elated about our future together.

Lastly, to my unborn children, words can't express the excitement I have waiting to meet you one day and seeing much of what God has placed in me materialize into a living, breathing, moving, walking, talking being that will continue to give the enemy hell for the cause of God's kingdom.

Introduction

My name is EDward Luis Long; however, I am affectionately known by many other names. To some as Kodi, others Young Dirty Bishop, to some as ED, and others ED Long, Jr. Now don't attempt to refer to me by any of the names listed if you don't know me as that individual. Each name represents a season of my life and I share a special bond with those who were with me in those seasons. Trust me, I will ignore you in the name of Jesus, lol. I am writing this book because no matter how you know me, personally, I am still known as the firstborn son of The Bishop Eddie Lee Long.

To many around the world, he is viewed as a spiritual leader, a transformational thinker, a general in God's kingdom, a spiritual father, a pastor, a brother, a friend, a confidant, an advisor, a husband, a son, or even a mentor and mentee, but to me, he is the only earthly father that I had or will have. My life has not been one that many would consider being normal and throughout my life, I have often been asked the question, "What is it like to be the son of Bishop Eddie L. Long?" My response has always been, "It's all I've ever known, so it's normal to me. I don't have anything to compare it to, because it's all I've ever known." To many who met him as a bishop, a pastor, an apostle, a frat brother, and so on, their perspective is just that to them, but to me, he's been my dad before he earned most of those titles. To be honest, many of those titles took away from and challenged his role in my life, while accentuating, enhancing, and aiding one of his most important titles, which was father.

In being a Pastor, he was serving the local church which caused him to be away a lot. As a reverend, he would be burning the midnight oil working on sermons. In becoming a bishop, he was called to the nation, and ultimately to the world. Others gravitated to him in awe of who he was in those roles. The other roles often took away from the role that was important to me, Father.

Since childhood I've grown into a young man who has been married, divorced, remarried, and now a father to be. I have ministered in pulpits and performed on stages around the world. I've hosted syndicated radio and television shows. I've won media, musical and philanthropic awards. I have two degrees and am pursuing another. In my own way, I am continuing what my father began and building on his legacy. Considering all of my milestones I don't feel that I have arrived. I consider myself a student of life and I'd like to share what I have learned while continually getting the revelation of lessons that my father was trying to teach me. Through my life experiences, I have matured in understanding things that previously I did not have the capacity to understand.

I want to challenge you to initially not read it from your perspective, but to truly hear my heart and aim to understand his heart in every story, passage, and scenario. From there, use these stories as a means for parenting or leading your household. If you are a young person who has a relationship with your parents, consider their wisdom and teaching as a blessing to help you develop into the best version of yourself.

Homecoming

Like many of my peers, I make up the portion of my generation whose parents were divorced and as a result, grew up in a single-parent household. I once took inventory of the familial status of my twelve closest friends and all of us were products of divorce. Wow! I don't have any memories of my parents being together. They divorced before I turned two years old, thus growing up in two different houses was my normal. We started out together in Fairburn, Georgia in a house they built together. That same house was the house they divorced in. Afterwards, my mother and I moved to a few different properties between East Point, Georgia and Riverdale, Georgia after their divorce. My dad found himself homeless for a short while until a lady gave him residence in a house in College Park, Georgia off of Creel Road.

In 1981, my mom was in Berean Christian Bookstore. In a very gentleman-type manner, Pastor Wilborn walked over and introduced himself to my mom only to discover that my mom and Pastor Wilborn's then fiancé were co-workers. Mrs. Angeletha and my mom were both flight attendants with the same airline. My mom enthusiastically shared with Pastor Wilborn that recently my pops had done his trial sermon at her home church. As a result, Pastor Wilborn invited my parents to his church service on the upcoming Sunday and soon afterwards Pop was licensed and ordained as an associate minister at Morning Star Baptist Church. This is the same place where my baby dedication service to The Lord was held.

Afterward, he took a senior pastoral position about two hours from where we lived in College Park, Georgia at Cedartown Baptist Church in Cedartown, Georgia. When I would visit my dad on the weekends, we would have what we called 'Friday Night Specials.' We would set up the video camera and record us having a good time. We would be dancing, singing, playing video games, and doing all kinds of fun stuff. Things were calmer on Saturday nights. Pop would work on his messages for the following Sunday late into the night while seated at the dining table. I would ask him the question, "What are you doing daddy?" He would always reply saying that he had work to do. Being a young child and not able to fully enunciate my words, I would reply that he was doing the "what to do." My God that would tickle him. Over the years that became a joke between us. From those days until his transition, that same regimen of studying and preparing on Saturday night continued. If I reached out to him on a Saturday and asked what he was doing, he would say he was doing the "what to do." As I continued to grow older, I recall a moment during one of my visits with my dad when he told me that one day my mom would give me to him. This moment was sometime shortly before I was to enroll in grade school. By this time, we had moved from College Park, Georgia over to Stone Mountain, Georgia because Pop had assumed the pastoral role at New Birth Missionary Baptist Church in Decatur, Georgia. It so happened that one of my visitation weekends was the registration period for DeKalb

County Schools. My mom and dad did not communicate much, if at all, so there wasn't a collective plan between them concerning my education. Both registered me for school. My mom registered me at E. W. Oliver Elementary School in Riverdale, Georgia and my dad took me to register at Woodridge Elementary School in Stone Mountain, Georgia. These schools were over 30 minutes away from each other.

Maybe he did it with the hope that mom did not have a plan or maybe he just did it as a backup in case something shifted. Nonetheless, he did it. As things normally flowed, my mom picked me up on the following Sunday night from his house and ultimately took me to the school she had registered me for. I remained at E. W. Oliver from kindergarten through third grade. While in third grade our student body was given a test. After taking that test, my mom was called to the school and informed about my results from the test. My performance on the assessment considered me to be gifted. The gifted program was developed for various students whose minds were highly creative and analytical. At that time X-Men was my favorite comic series. If you know anything about the X-Men, you know Charles Xavier founded a school for the gifted. The attendees had certain God-given supernatural and spiritual abilities in which they needed special attention and coaching. The results of this test proved I was truly an X-Man.

My mom bought me my first bicycle to celebrate the great news and her airline co-worker who was a Lockheed L-1011 Tristar plane mechanic taught how to ride it. After third grade, my mother and I moved to her hometown in North Carolina. Both my mother and father are from North Carolina, so we weren't moving to a foreign land. We were moving to be closer to family and have more financial stability. Though it was beneficial in some areas, it created more distance between my dad and me. This would directly impact the time I would be able to spend with him. We went from living about 35 minutes apart to now about 4.5 hours. We went from seeing each other every other weekend to now seeing each other maybe once a month, during the summers and on special holidays.

Over the years I had to adjust when coming to visit him. His time was becoming more limited due to this increasing success and impact as a pastor. The call and mandate on his life were growing. It was not strange for me to come visit him and he wouldn't be there. I began participating in a lot of church activities, getting transportation from some of my friends and leaders within the church, and charting my own way. I sometimes felt like I was raising myself.

My mom was a flight attendant which afforded me the privilege of flying non-revenue. When we moved to North Carolina, sometimes we would drive back to Atlanta, Georgia, but often I would fly by myself. Those were the good ole days before TSA was established. In those times anyone could walk into the airport and go directly to the gate. Looking back, that was a big risk for me to be traveling by myself as a child. All these things accelerated my growth. While living with my mom, my life and our means were very humble, initially living with my dad was the same. Over time he began to financially prosper. I began living in two different worlds at the same time. During my departure from my visitations with my dad he would remind me of what God told him. It was a statement that I held close.

While in fifth grade, in North Carolina, the school system decided to rezone the district which sent many of us who were living closer to the city out to a school in the more rural part of the county. This wasn't a good idea in my opinion, but it turned out to be a blessing in disguise. Our new school was predominantly Caucasian, and racism ended up being a big deal, especially for students of the African diaspora.

From day one I was having trouble with the transition. The only thing that I liked about the school was the football team. I struggled to connect with some of the students. I had this creative and gifted mind that had been exposed to much of the nation through experiences with both my mom and dad. I was a big city native trying to fit into a small town.

My new school wasn't challenging me academically and it was socially awkward. Going into the second month of the school year things were still not well. One day we were given a pop quiz. One of my African American classmates, whom I had a crush on, snatched my quiz from me. When she did that, I looked at her and said, "Why did you do that bitch?" Naturally, she something smart back to me. She also told the teacher what I said. I don't recall the teacher's name, but I do remember that she was an older Caucasian lady who looked very creepy to me. The teacher called me over to her desk and asked me what I said to the young lady. I informed her that I called my classmate a bitch because she snatched my paper from me. The teacher said, "Young man I'm going to have to write you up for that." And I told the teacher, "She could kiss my ass." As you can imagine, that escalated things to a different level. She escorted me from the classroom and took me directly to the principal's office. The principal of the rural elementary school was this tall, slim, older Caucasian man. He looked at me and told me that he had two choices. He could either whoop me or call my parents. I didn't respond to him. Somewhere in that exchange, he chose to call my mom.

My mom came to the school and was extremely disappointed. They informed her that I would be suspended from school and could return after three days. To be honest with you, I didn't care! None of this bothered me. I was only disappointed because it meant that I was going to miss football practice and may not remain on the team.

We got home that afternoon and my mom told me to go upstairs to our room. At that time, we were living with my grandparents and my mom and I shared a room upstairs, across the hallway from my grandparents. I spent a few hours in the room in solitude. She instructed me not to turn on the television or play any games. After some time she came upstairs and entered the room. She told me to grab her a belt. I complied. This was to be expected after getting suspended from school. She told me to turn around and she hit me with one lick, then another, and then a third. I was just standing there with my arms folded while looking out the window as she whipped me.

I was in fifth grade wearing a size 11 sneaker and standing at about five feet, seven inches. My mom was five feet even at best. She threw down the belt and began to cry saying this hurt her more than it hurt me. She was right! I could have taken another twenty-three licks and not been phased. She left the room and then the house. I don't recall much after this moment until later that night when she returned and told me to pack up all my stuff.

We moved a lot, so this was normal for me. From the time my parents got a divorce, between the two of their residences, I lived in about thirteen different places. I was accustomed to packing up and moving sporadically. I packed up my things, all my clothes, my wrestling men, my G.I. Joe action figures, my X-Men, my books, and sneakers. The following morning we loaded up the little two-door silver Mazda RX7 and hit the road.

We drove down I-85 and came back to Atlanta. Upon our arrival, we took residence at Motel 6 on Virginia Avenue in College Park, Georgia. While being in the motel, my mom called out to New Birth and asked to speak to my dad, to no avail. After being in the motel for about two days, I assume the frustration set it. We got in the car and drove from Virginia Avenue over to Stone Mountain, Georgia, where my dad lived in a neighborhood called Southland. Before going to his house, we stopped by Shadow Rock Elementary School where she registered me to complete my fifth-grade education.

Afterwards, we pulled up to the house and parked in the driveway. She told me to go up and ring the doorbell, so I did. I rang it a few times and no one came to the door and so I returned to the car. She then said to me, "Kodi, get your stuff and put it on the front porch. Tell your dad that I registered you for school and it's his turn to raise you." I thought she was joking, but when I looked at her, I knew she wasn't playing. She said to me that she had done the best that she could. She took me all around the country. She taught me how to read, write, how to get around and how to use the phone. I think that it's important for the youth to understand how important utilizing the phone was. When I was an adolescence the cellular phone hadn't been invented. The world was ignorant of smart phones. We only had house phones and public pay phones. My mom taught me how to utilize both. The time had come for my daddy to show me what she couldn't, how to be a man.

My mom never professed to be a prophet or anything of that nature, but at that moment she was being prophetic and incredibly wise. I did as she said. I grabbed my stuff and placed it on the porch. We hugged one another, and she said to me what she always said to me, "You know I love you right? Remember to always stop and think." That directive kept me from getting in more trouble than I had already gotten into. She then asked me to take her picture. My mom always kept cameras. I think that's where I got my affinity for pictures. I took her picture in front of the house and she left.

I don't remember what day of the week it was, but I sat on that porch for quite a while, growing restless. After getting tired from waiting, I walked up the street and knocked on a few of my friends' doors but no one was home. I went back to the house and just waited. Somewhere around the time of the sun going down, my dad pulled up in the driveway. He got out of the car and said, "Kodi? Kodi, what are you doing here?" I replied to him, "My mom said that she registered me for school and it's time for you to raise me." When I said that he broke down in the front yard crying like a baby. If you know anything about my dad, you know he never had any reservation about shedding a tear.

While crying, struggling to get himself together, he came over to give me a hug. He squeezed me so tight that he nearly killed me. He said, "Do you remember what I told you? One day!" He believed those words that God said to him, yet he was like the father of the mute boy at times. There were moments he had a little bit of disbelief. The father of the mute boy said, 'Lord I believe but can you help my unbelief,' according to Mark 9:23-24. A part of my dad's unbelief was shown when he tried to register me for kindergarten at Woodridge Elementary School. The registration could have been successful but that wouldn't have been what God said. When custody shifts there is a court process, or the child can choose when they become a certain age. We must be careful when we say what God said. Sometimes it's better that we don't say what God said if we're not totally committed to the process because it brings a different level of faith and accountability into the equation.

My father was telling me what our Father said to him. This presented a challenge for my dad. My dad was my father, but we were both sons of God. His demonstration on how to be an obedient son of God would have a major impact on my belief in God and how to remain faithful to His word. I was able to watch my father wrestle with letting God do what He said that He would do in His own time and way. You best believe it has helped me to stick to the course, stick to the script, stick to the plan, and stick to trusting God's word whenever I hear him say something.

The way we respond in our obedience and our follow through to the instructions of God lays a blueprint for others who are watching us. It also increases their faith that God is real, and God is true. Being able to see a process where God said and did to and for them what he said he was going to do, creates a higher aptitude of faith. Say this with me, "I know that He can and will do the same for me."

Faith isn't about being perfect; it's about being persistent that when we make a move, choice, or decision that's anti to our faith, all we have to do is repent, reposition, and get back on our faith path. In this section I would like for you to write down the things you have heard God say to you, promises He's given you, and instructions He's given to you.

Write down when you heard him say it and where you were when you heard him say it.

REFLECT NOW...

Things God Said to Me:

Promises God Gave to Me:

God's Instructions for Me:

Just to document and consider, what were some of the things you were about to do to attempt to take matters into your own hands? Ask yourself if you have enough faith to tear up that plan and stick to His? I used to hear my grandmother and grandfather say they were just going to let God have his way. That statement is so much easier said than done, especially in a world where we want to have control, input, and influence not only over the outcome but also the process. Can we let go and let God? I don't know what God said to my mom, but I know that what she said was true. She had given me her best and it was time to turn me over. Maybe God told her to do that. Maybe he gave her a different promise. Sometimes we can become so anxious to see God do something that we take into our own hands. This can delay what only God can do. Many of us are stopping someone else's process because God can't get to them until we get out of the way. Let go and let God.

Secure the Bag

In my preteen or early adolescent years, I was really struggling to identify my place. As a young man growing up with a single mom, as well as with a newlywed father, traveling back and forth from Georgia to North Carolina was too much. I was also faced with another dynamic. While living with my mom in North Carolina, we stayed in a small town, but my grandfather was referenced as the Unofficial Black Mayor. He was an entrepreneur, a decorated WWII Veteran, a deacon at his church, and a philanthropist. In Atlanta, my father was emerging to the national and global scene, as a minister and revolutionary. It's safe to say there was pressure on both ends to be smart, honorable, and well-behaved, but at the same time, I was just a kid who was trying to figure out how to balance my life.

My mom and I moved around a lot as her income was not high, yet she was fighting to provide me with the best life she could. During my visitations with my dad, I had to adjust from all of my time being spent with him, to him now traveling frequently, and me not seeing him much during those times with him. On top of all that, I just wanted a sense of belonging...to be cool and fit in with my peers. I think I have always been able to find a way to relate to a broad spectrum of people because I had been exposed to a plethora of experiences.

In some of the upcoming chapters, I will dispel portions of the myth that I was raised with a silver spoon in my mouth. If anything, my life began with the same spoon as everyone else, then shifted to a plastic or wooden spoon, followed by juggling that same plastic spoon with trying to learn how to use a silver spoon. At this point of my life, I'm referencing when I was 11 or 12 years old, I felt like Will Smith. Some days living in West Philadelphia, while other days felt like I was in Beverly Hills. Now Will moved from one setting to the next, permanently, versus me going back and forth weekly. Again, it was hard to find stability in one place or the other.

While in fifth grade, at Shadowrock Elementary

School in Stone Mountain, Georgia, I continued to get in fights and emerged as the class clown. I found ungainful employment by serving as a distraction to my teacher and hindering her from reaching her goal, which was to educate us all. It came to a point where she was just downright done with me, but the God in her chose to call my dad versus writing me up. During that moment, I wasn't really feeling her but, in the moments to come, I learned to appreciate her. Though my dad moved around and traveled a lot with meetings and orchestrating things, for the most part when he could, he would stop what he was doing to see about me, especially when called upon.

During this incident with my teacher, he came to the school for an impromptu parent-teacher-student meeting. If you have ever been in this type of disciplinary meeting, you know how this goes. It starts off with the teacher acting all nice toward the parent while expressing the undesirable behaviors of the student. She tells my dad the story of how I had been, "showing out for attention with my classmates," and how she had been more than lenient towards me, but she felt more disciplinary action was needed. Step two always comes where the parent asks the child, "Is there anything you have to say for yourself?" I hated that pseudo-court of law session which never seemed to work in my favor. So of course, I said, "I don't have anything to say." In all my life, my dad has only given me about three whippings. He often shared that I was the child who all he had to do was to talk and for the most part, I would adjust and straighten up. It was just the kind of rapport he had with me. In this instance he asked my teacher to step out of the room for a moment, she obliged.

I did not know where he was going or where he was coming from, but on this particular day in an 8.5 by 11-inch manilla envelope, he just happened to have a lot of money on him. We were sitting in this cold, quiet, closet-size office, and he told me to look at him. While I'm looking at him, he begins talking and pulls out this folder, and puts it in my hand. I open up the folder after he instructs me to, and he tells me to pull out the money and lay it on the desk. I took the money out and laid it on the desk and he said to me, "Do you know how much money that is?" and I said to him, "Uhh, no." His next words to me were, "Son, that is $15,000."

My granddad kept a wallet on him, and we used to go and steal money out of it, 'Lord forgive me.' He would have a couple of hundred dollars in there, maybe ten one-hundred-dollar bills, give or take, and we thought he was rich. So, to see $15,000, my mind was blown away. My dad tells me to look at him again and while I'm looking at him, I will never forget that moment... Life is not all about money and he says, "Son, I don't want you to jeopardize your life and all that God has for you by showing out in school and in class. You're here to learn so you can do what God will have for you to do in your life. I asked you to count the money so you can get a glimpse of what your future can look like."

And to this day, I don't know why but I just started crying as he was talking to me. I don't know if it was his affirming my potential...I don't know if it was him helping me to dream. I don't know if it was because I was feeling ashamed. I don't know why, but I do know that I just started crying as if he had given me a whipping. He gave me a hug and held me as I was crying. From that moment on, I think I begin to adjust almost everything about myself. I believe that moment helped me to begin to value myself and value what I could accomplish in life. I didn't walk away feeling like I was worth or not worth $15,000, or that I was going to have $15,000 one day. I just walked away feeling valued.

Even in my adult life, I think about that moment quite often. As I previously stated, I'm grateful for my teacher and how she handled it because she could have written me up which would have been on my school record. I'm even more grateful for how my dad responded. I had my share of whippings from pretty much all of my more senior family members and none of those whippings had ever made me feel valuable. Sure, my dad could have whipped me right there; being embarrassed because he was a pastor in the city and he had to come up to the school because his son was showing out, while he's helping youth and young adults all throughout the city and preaching the gospel on Sundays. Wow, I never really thought about what it was like for him to come up to the school until right now.

In all of that, instead of whipping me, he chose to affirm me, and instead of doing what everyone else had done before by putting a switch to my tail, he chose to look introspectively to identify what the root issue was. He identified the weeds that were restricting my growth and he chose to uproot the weeds and fertilize the good seeds.

As parents who are reading this now, once more, I challenge you to identify what your child needs and what your child is missing versus instinctively resorting to physical reprimands which may only provide a temporary resolution. Jesus was on the earth as our brother, but also as a representative of our heavenly father. There was a time when Peter got out of line. Peter's actions and his words were not aligned with who he was really called to be. Jesus looked at Peter and said, "get back Satan." Meaning as a friend, brother, and representing the father, He was able to call the Christ in Peter up while calling the negative spirit that was trying to consume Peter out.

Jesus then tells us that these things and greater things we will do. This means we all have the ability to call our sons and our daughters into what they're supposed to be while calling them out of any wrongdoings they are entangled in. I challenge us all, not only when we talk to our children, but even as we talk to one another, family, friends, spouses, associates, employees, and employers that instead of chastising one another let us move with compassion as my father did, calling one another up and into our respectful destinies as we call each other out of what has had a hold on us.

REFLECT NOW...PARENTS

1. How do you respond to your children when they get out of line?

2. Do you discipline them with or without explanation, clarity, and instruction?

3. Do you respond to your children's actions emotionally or do you think through your response before responding?

4. What outcome do you want from disciplining your children?

5. Have you expressed this to them?

6. Have you affirmed your Children and their future?

7. Are you receptive to the manner in which your parents' discipline you?

8. Is there another way that your parents could discipline you that would be more affective?

9. Have you expressed this to them?

10. What are some changes that you can make so that your parents don't have to discipline you?

SexED

When I was a 6th Grade student at Shadowrock Elementary School in Stone Mountain, Georgia, and now living with my dad, my grade level was invited to take sexual education classes at Fernbank Science Museum. As rambunctious little preteens, we referred to Fernbank as Spermbank Science Museum.

I remember my teacher, Ms. Kreminsky, who was this short, four-and-a-half foot, Caucasian, 20-something-year-old teacher of mine that I had a crush on, came into our class announcing it. It's funny because it was difficult not only for the students but for the faculty to distinguish her from the students because she was so small that she just blended in with us. When I was in sixth grade, I was wearing a size 12 sneaker, standing 5'7", and during that time the box haircut was the style that made me look even taller. I remember her walking into the classroom and trying to call us to attention. If truth be told, I wasn't the only young man in the class that had a crush on her and as kids, we would be a little bit more combative with a person that we were crushing on than with somebody that we really did not care that much about, so she always got our attention. She made an announcement that we had an opportunity to take part in this new sexual education class that was a partnership between DeKalb County Schools and the Fernbank Science Museum.

Everybody was intrigued, excited, and even tickled about the choice of words she had to use in explaining the program making us aware that we would learn about our sexual organs, the sexual organs of the opposite gender, and more. While loading the buses to head home that afternoon, many students were excited about attending the program and the possibility of seeing friends from other schools and wondered if they would be going at the same time as us. I even wondered if my friends from church, who attended other schools, were invited to go as well. We received forms and were instructed to take them home to our parents, read them over with our parents and have our parents sign the form giving us permission to attend the sexual education classes. I got home and I can't remember whether or not it was that night or the next, but at some point, I did get a chance to mention it to my dad and bring it to his attention. I recall very vividly him saying "no!" Mind you at this point my other friends had spoken to their parents and had gotten their forms signed saying that they could go and they were excited about it.

Now I must be transparent with you in stating that by the time I was in sixth grade, I probably didn't need much sex education. I watched my first porno when I was four years old and I had some other preteen sexual encounters that I will share at another time. I'd kissed girls and done other things with them. We had a game that we would play, that you may be familiar with, which was the freaky version of Hide and Go Seek, entitled Hide and Go Get It. When the family was around, we would play hide and go seek but when adults went away, we would play hide and go get it. Even growing up in church, in the middle of worship services and bible studies, while we were supposed to be hearing the word of God, there's no telling what we would be up to.

So taking these sexual education classes probably would have just given me more tools and education to use in ways that weren't the best for me. I was simply excited and wanted to go because this was like the new and cool thing to do and would be the place to be. When my dad told me no, I was devastated because I just knew he would say yes. I remember asking him why and he told me something very simple but profound. It was very profound back in the mid-'90s, but it's even more profound now in the 2020s. He stated that it was his job to teach me about sex, and if I had any questions concerning or about sex, I could come to him and talk about it. He was not entrusting my sexual education to the school system and to people he did not know, nor did he know their belief systems.

As a 6th grader, my mind was focused on having a good time, having fun with my friends, and possibly learning a few things. But my dad was taking leadership as a father and a prophet. My dad was preaching some of his most infamous sermons during that time. Some of you should remember; if you don't, feel free to purchase some of his books and sermons from the 90s. Books like *I Don't Want Delilah, I Need You*, or *What A Man Wants, What A Woman Needs*, where he talked about the purpose of sex, the purpose of the family, abstinence, and celibacy.

As a pastor or believers in Jesus, many of us teach things that we don't really apply in our own households or live by. Many of us say stuff that's just cliché or we make things a trend like they are just the flavor of the month. We don't really take them as convictions within our own hearts and allow our decisions to be led by those convictions. Let's break this down. Not only was my dad saying no to me going, but he was also saying no to the emerging world systems. His posture was saying if we're not going to be on the same page in the standards, we're training our youth, then I don't want my son to be a part of this. You all may be teaching him that he has a choice of what gender he wants to be, or you may be exposing him to things he hasn't thought about, and it may be too early for my son to consider these things. It's also a challenge that may be the school system should talk to the parents before presenting this to the students, versus just sending a letter home and expecting parents to conform to the pressures of others.

There are so many things I imagined he was considering in simply saying "no, you can't go to that." But he didn't just necessarily take something away and leave it at that, nor did he offer an alternative, rather he blocked something and offered the source. I want you to follow me on that.

A father gives direction and identity. I have never struggled with identity issues because it was confirmed out of my father's mouth versus going to an educational place or other places and being presented with other options that could have been given to me which could have led to me now questioning my identity down the line. Pop created an open-door policy for me to come to talk to him about sex and receive continual affirmation. The source of our identity comes from our father or our parents if you will, and our heavenly father. The enemy or world systems try to present alternatives as if they are the source. If we send our youth to school to get their foundation for learning, then we have replaced the home with the school. The home should be the place of first love, first encounter, and first instruction. At one time there weren't schools; there was just the house that scaled into schools.

To say no was to signify that the educational program wasn't my primary source; my father was my primary source, and I could come to him for that information. When the enemy approached Adam and Eve and offered them to eat off the tree of knowledge of good and evil, he was exposing them to some things that God never intended for them to explore. God gave them everything and said it was good. He showed them the good and only how to work the things for the good. The enemy exposed all of humanity to the bad.

My father was positioned to show me the good

things about sex like how to wait for it, identify a spouse, being prepared for a family, and the overall benefits of sex. But it's the enemy's job to expose us to the bad aspects of sex like pornography, exploitation, non-consensual sex, and all other things that were not a part of God's original design. Yes, temporarily it caused me to be embarrassed and my friends to say, "man, what's up, why aren't you going?" It caused for my cool card to be challenged, but I'm thankful that my father stood and practiced what he preached in his home, as well as what he was sharing from the pulpit. Had he conformed, I may not be who I am today. We are in an age where many are conforming sexually, falling below God's standards, and accepting whatever man's standards are. I am blessed to have been raised in the right way. I am even more appreciative of this memoir during these current, critical times.

REFLECT NOW...PARENTS

1. What educational programs are you or your child exposed to now? Are they based on Godly principles or based on worldly things?

2. What have you not shared with your children that could help them?

3. What questions do you think your children may have for you concerning their identities that you can answer for them?

4. This is a lesson that my dad taught me in the mid-90s. Now here we are, present day, facing these challenges, opportunities, and more so knowing the current conditions of the world...

   a. What are some things that you need to talk to your children about and haven't and why haven't you?

   b. Do you know what to say to them?

   c. Are you fearful of society rejecting you?

    d. Are you wrestling with love versus acceptance?

REFLECT NOW...ADOLESCENTS

1. What are some questions you have for your parents concerning your identity or concerning their experiences?

2. What are some things that you would like for your parents to be transparent with you about concerning their own sexual challenges and/or choices, decisions, or opportunities?

3. How do you feel knowing these things will help you?

4. Who do you view as your source for sexual information and development? Where do you think that you should go for this type of training and/or teaching?

Houston, We Have a Problem!

You know, in the great state of Texas, they do everything BIG. Big houses, big cars, big trucks, big animals, and when they eat, they eat big. My dad had to preach out in Houston, Texas and he decided to take me with him. I didn't get to travel with my dad on his engagements as often as I would have liked, so you can imagine how overjoyed I was whenever he took me with him. I was roughly eleven or twelve years old and he took me on this trip out to Houston, where he was scheduled to speak at The Brentwood Missionary Baptist Church, which the great Reverend Joseph Ratliff pastored. I'd known Pastor Ratliff, affectionately "Uncle Joe," my whole life as he and my father met at Interdenominational Theological College when I was young. He'd preached for my dad over the years and my dad had preached at the church he pastored.

Growing up, we took a few family trips to Houston and we would stay with Uncle Joe Ratliff and his wife from time to time. I have a lot of fond memories of going to Houston and hanging out with Uncle Joe. I remember Uncle Joe taking us to the Astrodome on a tour back when the Tennessee Titans football team were the Houston Oilers. We also took a few trips to Six Flags AstroWorld. He's a very caring man, one of those guys whose presence is immediately felt when he walks in the room. He's a comedian, gentleman, and showman, but yet he loves the Lord, and you can feel the love of God in his presence.

One night when we were out in Houston on this ministry trip, Uncle Joe invited us to join him for dinner. Now remember, I said Texas does everything big. He picked us up from our hotel and took us on a fine dining experience. We arrived at a big restaurant, whose name I don't recall, but they had big lobsters in the tanks when we walked in and it was crowded from what I recall.

Like any dinner, we sat down and socialized for a while. Remember now, I was eleven or twelve years old, so I was still to be seen and not heard if you will. During that time it was fine with me because I was simply happy to be there. Being around the adults at the table afforded me a chance to be exposed to different things and grow up a little quicker by hearing their conversations and being introduced to ideas that most kids my age weren't. When it came time for us to place our meal order, I remember Uncle Joe specifically looking at me with that big smile of his and saying, "Kodi, order whatever you want."

Now you know good and well, you can't take a kid anywhere in the world; not to a toy store, amusement park, clothing store, candy store, or a restaurant and tell them to order whatever they want. I took his words to heart and perused around that menu. I believed this was the first time I looked at a menu and saw the word market next to an item. I didn't know what the word market meant. Everything else had a dollar sign and some numbers next to it but the whole lobster had the word market next to it. I thought, "Aha, I've never had a whole lobster at a restaurant like this and these lobsters put the lobsters that I'm used to seeing at Red Lobster to shame."

Now from a contextual standpoint, I want you to understand my life at that time. I had just moved in with my dad. As I stated, my mom had dropped me off to stay with him (that's another chapter we have to talk about). While living with my mom, we moved around a lot. We had been evicted from places and meals weren't as lavish, nor easy to come by. As a single mom, she did the best that she could, but five-star restaurants were definitely not normal for us. My mom tried to expose me to good dining at that time by going to places like Olive Garden, Houston's, and other restaurants, yet when we would go, we weren't ordering meals. We knew how to be in the building, look nice and get full for about five or so dollars by ordering multiple orders of the salad, along with bread and splitting an appetizer at best. You may recall yourself doing this from time to time.

We would go to Olive Garden and order the $2.70 salad bowl with unlimited refills coupled with the Italian breadsticks for another two or so dollars with unlimited refills. Can I get a Hallelujah? From the times that we would go to Red Lobster and order the garlic biscuits and split a shrimp pasta, I knew the lobsters at Red Lobster looked nothing like the lobsters at that restaurant with Uncle Joe that night. I had never had this kind of offer on the table before and didn't know when I would receive another one so when that man told me to order anything I wanted, you bet Bon Appetit. They do it big in Texas, so I was going to do it big with those big old lobsters.

I ordered the lobster, and it came with a lot of extra food. The lobster was the main attraction, but the supporting cast wasn't a letdown. It came with warm sides and all kinds of delectables. I ate as much of it as I could but honestly that meal was for a grown man and my eleven- or twelve-year-old self didn't even eat half of it. I boxed the remains to go with a satiated smile. Of course, all good things must come to an end. It became time for us to go back to our hotel, as service was going to be the next day, and everyone needed their rest to be prepared to preach and worship the Lord together.

Uncle Joe dropped us off at our hotel and my dad and I walked into the hotel to get on the elevator. As soon as the elevator doors closed, Houston, we have a problem! Now, my dad loved the Lord and I don't think there's any question about that, but in his messages, he began being known as the 'cussing preacher' over the years. Sometimes he would say things like, 'We're going to give the devil hell,' or he would begin to make a statement, pause, and say... "You know what I meant right there" and the congregation would laugh knowing exactly what he was saying. At this moment in the elevator no sooner than the doors closed, I got my sermon for that trip a little early. He looked at me and said, "Son, don't you ever order anything that your ass can't pay for yourself." You can imagine the emotional swing I was on, as I had my leftovers in my hand, stomach full, and smiling having never eaten a meal at market price. The plans of going to bed dreaming about what our post-service meal, on the next day, would even be like was removed from my thoughts, as all of the air was released from my hot balloon with my dad's statement.

As we exited the elevator and walked down the hall, he said "It is disrespectful to order meals that aren't in your own budget." He pointed out he didn't order anything extravagant, so I had no business ordering anything extravagant. He said that Uncle Joe was just being nice in what he said and that it's customary to say, "Order whatever you want," when you're hosting a dinner. He told me, "You never order more or beyond what the host orders." This was a lot to take in for an 11 or 12-year-old, but I guess he figured I was mature enough to receive it. He also got on me because I didn't finish my meal. He said I was eating with my eyes and not with my stomach, and there was no way in the world I was that hungry because we had already eaten two other times that day.

My dad was always big on respect. He had worked a lot of jobs and didn't get many handouts. He found elevation from service, through consistency and God's grace. He wasn't one to use or exploit people, but he knew how to utilize people. My dad made sure I developed those same traits and characteristics. There were a lot of lessons at that dinner. As I have grown and gone through life, I have never forgotten the lesson my dad taught me that night. When I'm hosted at dinner, I order what is in my budget so if push comes to shove, I can pay for it. I have also learned to observe what the host orders and about the range of price the host meal falls within. As an adult who is a little more liberal in my beverage choice, if someone invites me out, particularly clergy, if I don't see them order a glass of wine or what have you, then I won't. I have come to understand what we eat, how we eat, where we eat, and when we eat, all of those things say a lot about us, and people pay attention to those things. A lot of business is done at the table and people make decisions based upon how you behave yourself over a meal.

I have been on dates with young ladies that I initially really liked, but that first date ended up being the only date because of certain things they had done. They were like the 11 or 12-year-old me by ordering things that were extravagant knowing they would not do that on their own account. Those were signs to me that this person may be one that will attempt to take advantage of me.

To all my sisters who are reading this book, single and searching for love, this is a moment where you can evaluate yourself with someone who wants to spend their life with you... If they can easily observe that you are one that can easily take advantage of them or maybe you're not taking advantage of them and it's just a budgeting thing, they will look and say this person is not really considering me and my budget. There are a lot of questions that can come up concerning our decision-making, our respect level, and our aptitude simply by sitting down and having a meal. Many friendships have been broken up because friends would go on trips together or go out to eat together and one may not have the funds and may not say it until the end of the meal, knowing good and well that they did not have the money the whole time leaving the other(s) to cover their meal or accommodations. This makes me think about the point that my dad made again when he said, 'Don't order what your ass can't pay for."

One of the last engagements Jesus had with the disciples was The Last Supper. This was a time of communion, but it also was a time of instruction. When we sit down at the 'table of brotherhood,' as Dr. King described it, this is the time where we really learn about one another and about ourselves. The next time you sit down at a table with anyone, consider them just as much as you consider yourself when breaking bread.

Boom!

If I didn't state it earlier or if you haven't put it together by now, I grew up in the city that's too busy to hate, Atlanta, Georgia, Shawty; A-T-L h*e! The home of the booty clubs, Freak-Nik, and the capital of the Bible belt. Atlanta is also the urban music capital of the world, home of the world's busiest airport, the epicenter of civil rights, and is also known as Black Hollywood. Atlanta is the headquarters of the Dirty South and Trap Music movements. After receiving the honor of hosting the 1996 Olympics, largely due to the hard work of many African Americans, including the late Maynard Jackson, Andrew Young, H.J. Russell, and many others, Atlanta became the mecca for not only Black People but unique individuals with a dream. Thus, truly positioning us to make an imprint in the earth when the Olympics were brought to Atlanta, there was so much excitement by all of us ATLiens. We started seeing buildings being built, stadiums being constructed, and people from all over the world beginning to move here. Our church, where membership was already high, even experienced more of a boom in weekly attendance and membership.

Being a teen at this time, I became exposed to business contracts and people getting themselves in positions as vendors for many of the games that were going to take place in a few years. I remember my dad working hard to position the church and its members to get vendor contracts or part-time jobs which turned into longer employment and careers for some. A lot of the vendors were paying teenagers between $15 - $20 an hour which was like a million dollars to us back then. It was an overly exciting, engaging, and impactful time here in Atlanta. With all the business that was taking place, there was a strong desire to attend one of the Olympic matches. Not everyone was able to attend because tickets were awfully expensive and sparse, yet fast forward from the announcement of the Olympics to the actual Olympics taking place, we were blessed enough to get tickets to attend an Olympic match.

My dad had been building relationships with many athletes during this era. Players like Otis Nixon and Brian Jordan of the Atlanta Braves, Deion Sanders aka Primetime of the Atlanta Falcons, Evander "Real Deal" Holyfield, and many others. He had also begun building a relationship with Shaquille O'Neal who was on the 1996 USA Basketball Dream Team (Part Three). On July 27, 1996, we attended an exhibition match between the Dream Team and China. There's no need for me to say it because you already know that the Dream Team demolished them. Anyone attending the game was not going to see a highly competitive match, but you were going to see the best players in the NBA, all on the court at the same time, filming a highlight reel.

After the game, we had passes to attend a special post-game meet and greet dinner with the players at the Omni Hotel, which was right across from the Georgia Dome and the Omni Arena. Can you imagine being a teenager in the room with all these star basketball players? I was living it up! Feel me, I was living it UP! We're eating great food, taking pictures, and getting autographs. It was great!

My dad blows my high by saying to me, "Kodi, we're going to leave soon. I just feel like we need to go on and get out of here." You can imagine that leaving and going home was the last thing that I had on my mind. We had only been in the room for about 30 to 45 minutes and some of the players were still coming in. I think that only David Robinson, John Stockton, Hakeem Olajuwon, and Shaquille O'Neal were in the room at this time. The night was still young and all of the players had not entered the room yet.

Now if you know anything about my father you knew he was definitely led by The Holy Spirit and a lot of times he would move based on what he called "unctions." My dad was a very smart and insightful man to whom God also revealed a lot of things to. Because of this, people oftentimes asked the questions, "What was Bishop's marketing plan? What was his plan for this? Structure for that?" They would ask him these questions expecting a very robust and detailed strategic response. Often, they would be disappointed because his response would be, "I just follow the Holy Spirit. I get an unction and I move on it." The fact is true that most of the prolific things he's done, that so many marvel at, were based on unctions which he had.

This night, as I stated before, he had an unction that was contrary to my desires. I didn't want to leave as I had been looking forward to that night for a long time and all of a sudden, we had to roll out because he had an unction. So, we leave and make our way to the car. As we're doing so, he called my bonus mother and told her we were about to head home. We got in the car and drove out of the deck of the Omni hotel and past the all-new Centennial Olympic Park, where we saw many people enjoying themselves. We float through the city and merge onto I-20 and as we're driving, he cuts on the radio to a talk radio show. Although I've done hip-hop, college, and gospel radio, many people don't know this, but one of my dreams is to actually do talk radio. I think I picked this up because Pop would always listen to talk radio in the car, helping him to stay informed.

As we're listening to the radio station, the announcer interrupts the normal broadcast and reports, "Breaking news, breaking news, a bomb has just gone off in Centennial Park. We cannot confirm right now how many were harmed or injured, but we can confirm that a bomb just exploded in Centennial Park." At that moment, ML, my younger brother Jared, and my sister Taylor were at the house. My dad and I were in the car having just rode past where the bomb exploded. It was quiet in the car for a moment and I started to think, "Wow, we could have gotten killed down there tonight." My dad did not say anything. It's important for you to know that this was also a Saturday night which meant that the next day was Sunday service. During this time in 1996, New Birth was on a trajectory to reach its peak. We were having three packed services, in a 3,500-seat sanctuary, hosting roughly 10,000 people per Sunday, not to mention the overflow. The first service kicked off about 6:30 am and the last did not end until about 2:00 pm or later.

Pop would be up until about 1:00 am or 2:00 am in the morning on Saturday nights, preparing and studying. I imagined he did that either before or planned on doing it after the game. My point is that I know that the next day had to be on his mind and so I believe there were two things working in tandem on that night. I'm convinced neither of us wanted to leave the meet and greet. Being in that environment was a once-in-a-lifetime experience. I can only imagine how difficult it was for him to tell his son, "I know we just got here, but we have to go." I am clear that my dad received the unction that we needed to leave. On top of that, his devotion to his life's calling and being prepared for ministry could also lead him to say, "I need to make sure I'm in position and prepared to minister to God's people in the morning."

As I stated before, he would be up just as late on Saturday nights as we were when this bomb went off a little after 1:00 am. He's had to be at events on

Saturday nights that would have him out even later than this time, but he had this unction that we needed to leave. The narrative could have possibly been different with ML, Jared, and Taylor waking up the next morning to their husband, son, and brother being hospitalized or even worse if it weren't for that unction. The narrative could have been where someone had to walk to the pulpit to say, "Be in prayer for Bishop Long and Edward" but he chose to move at the unction of the Holy Spirit to get us out of harm's way and to be mindful that his life's calling wasn't to be in a room with athletes just enjoying himself, but as he oftentimes had said, "I have a charge to keep and a God to glorify." Being driven by purpose would not allow him to be distracted by pleasure.

I want to pause right here because there's something in that for all of us. I have had moments where I've ended up in some mess even though I knew it was time to leave the party; I knew it was time to leave the club, I knew it was time to leave my friend's house, I knew it was time, where I just would get that feeling, that unction but I would choose pleasure over purpose. In some of those incidents, I've ended up getting robbed, getting in a fight, pulled over by the police, and losing something, because I temporarily lost sight of my purpose by being blinded by pleasure.

The word of the Lord says obedience is better than sacrifice. What situations have you found yourself in that you've looked back and said, "I had no business being in that situation but I chose not to listen to that still, quiet voice of the Holy Spirit." As I got older, there were many times I reflected on how my dad showed me how to hear and feel these unctions of the Holy Spirit and how to move on them. God put my dad and me in a situation that could have presented a different outcome. My dad taught me many lessons but teaching me how to get up from the table, walk away from the stars and bright lights, and not be distracted while having the strength to stick to the course, is amongst the greatest.

I want to encourage you in the same way. Ladies as you're reading this, this may keep you from getting raped by not being in the wrong situation and leaving when it's time to leave. Fellas this can keep you from being locked up. I've coached and counseled people that were in jail because they were hanging with some people and got that feeling or unction that it was time to leave but they chose to stay. They did not want to miss out on something and by not wanting to miss out, they ended up getting everything that came with the situation. Sometimes it's okay to tip out the room with your church finger up and read about the rest on social media. We don't have to be at every event or involved in everything or be the life of every party. I began to develop a rule for myself; I'm never the first there and never the last to leave. The following Sunday, Pop was able to stand in the pulpit offering prayers for the families that were affected by the bomb explosion and offering support and resources to the city. He was able to stand in his purpose because he wasn't distracted by pleasure. Keep standing y'all.

<u>REFLECT NOW...</u>

1. What are some things, people, or situations that are currently distracting you?

2. Who is depending on you to make spirit-led decisions?

3. What are your guilty pleasures? What purposeful activities can you replace them with?

More with Les

I am writing this chapter on May 30, 2020, from Atlanta in the aftermath of Friday night protests focusing on justice for George Floyd and his untimely and unnecessary murder. Last night, I witnessed a collection of people representing different nationalities, ethnic backgrounds, races, and gender, primarily from the millennial, Y, and Z generations, in pain and utter disbelief. Through moments of deep anger and unbridled aggression, what began as a positive and peaceful demonstration, turned into violent, physical altercations with the Atlanta Police Department that escalated into the destruction of African American-owned properties and businesses of innocent parties.

Much of what we saw displayed goes back to parenting. Although many children are sent to school to learn, some are taught and trained about various things at church, and some participate in other programs to increase exposure. The majority of a child's learning takes place in the home; what is demonstrated is then vested in the child. The right attention is especially important.

Words of affirmation lead to self-worth. Understanding of value is then reciprocated to others. Proper demonstration leads to emulation because we emulate what we see. I want you to understand what I'm saying. What we put in ourselves, we regurgitate, so what is invested in a child is what will come out of a child.

God made man in his image because he wanted humanity to understand and demonstrate the power that we see God demonstrate as our Creator. This has given us creative ability; we see God speak and see things happen so that we then can speak and see things happen. The images that a child sees are the things a child turns and does. As I watched the riots and looting across various cities across these pseudo-United States, I had to ask myself where was this behavior learned from? Racism is not a naturalistic way of thinking and way of being, yet it's taught, therefore a learned behavior. Is the looting mindset rooted in taking something out of anger? It was upsetting to see many of my peers, and other generations, acting this way. Not only was I upset to witness their behavior, but it was also more upsetting to question the motivation behind their actions. I believe this behavior is learned from somewhere.

For parents who may feel ill-equipped to raise their children, experience regrets bringing a life into this world and not knowing what to do or feel like a failure for not having the capacity to be responsible for your offspring, I want you to know that it's not over. I want to share a story with you of how my father felt in some ways similar to you but came to a resolve that sometimes we can do more with less.

Between my senior year in high school and my early years in college, my dad and I weren't connecting on certain things. He was mentoring and helping others, while I felt I wasn't getting the attention I needed. His intentionality for supporting others, I felt I needed. My dad was a great provider, which was something he felt he never received from his father and his father did not feel he received from his father. The provision he provided us positioned him to feel successful within himself. But with new levels come new devils, and often the bigger we are, the more room and more space we have for oversight.

In focusing on the bigger picture, some of the basics were overlooked. Though I knew my dad's heart, sometimes I felt I was a casualty of his service to others. What I desired was the intentionality I saw some of the ministry auxiliaries and mentees receiving. As time went on, there was a disconnect; my dad wasn't really understanding who I was or who I was becoming. I have always been an honest person in telling folks who I am and what I am about without any shame in making that announcement. During this time, my artistry name was 'Dirty Bishop' and I held no qualms about it. My teammate Stephen Tookes was the one who donned me with that name while going to football practice one day at Stephenson High School. He used to call me 'The Bishop' and one day he said, "it's the Dirty Bishop!" and the name stuck. The name was so proper because I was always viewed by my peers as the righteous guy out of the group, but I was also the "turn up" guy. I was in the thick of my days of exploring opportunities with the opposite sex, going to parties, and just living a carefree life. I was promiscuously righteous, and I fully embodied this oxymoronic statement.

During my high school years, I got into communications with our close circuit television network being the sports anchor and editor. During my days at FAMU, I had one of the crunkest radio shows in the city of Tallahassee. Not only did I play inspirational vitamins, provide conscious content, I also promoted ratchet activities and music. I was unapologetically me. As I transitioned from being in my father's house to being away at college, physical distance added to the space that was already there. My dad was traveling a lot during my senior year in high school responding to the global call on his life. Now, I was four hours away from home, sowing wild oats, while earning an education.

Around my freshman/sophomore year, Pop invited a prolific and world-renowned speaker to facilitate a revival and to present a different way of understanding God's kingdom and its power. Pop told me he wanted me to be there, so I was present and to my surprise, this prolific, world-renowned, thought-provoking, called-to-action speaker was none other than Mrs. Mamie Brown's baby boy, Mr. Leslie (Les) Brown.

I want to pause for a moment and set the stage for you, to help you understand how much of a game-changer this move was. I know that now it is very common for us to see speakers, artists, and the likes standing in pulpits and on platforms in churches but during this time that was not common, and Pop was one of the first to do this. To have a motivational speaker who was in the ranks of Jim Rohn, Bob Proctor, Tony Robbins, and others to be standing in a pulpit for a series of days to revive and provoke innovative thoughts and beliefs, was an experience; Mr. Brown did not disappoint. He, like my dad, has the natural ability to advance the

Kingdom of God through unorthodox means. So that my friends, I did get naturally.

After one of the services, Pop brought Mr. Brown and me together. He told Mr. Brown that he was watching me during the service and was able to see how his words were resonating within me. The reason that is important is I had been in church my whole life, seen a lot, and most times would sit there and not really pay attention. I was more so a participant observer, rather than an active listener. ML and I were talking recently, and she reminded me how she would go to my dad and say, "Kodi's not paying attention in service. He's there, but you need to talk to him. He's not clapping like everyone else or shouting Amen." But over the years, she came to the understanding that I was always focused. She sees now that my demonstration of my faith is evidenced by my ability to regurgitate what I picked up.

My dad noticed something similar and how I did not really respond to the many prolific ministers who had come and spoken over the years, but yet there was something within Les Brown that demanded a response out of me without even trying. He said to both of us while standing in his office, that he noticed there was a connection there. Here is a revered man, who put his son's growth and matriculation, above his pride, to ask another man to mentor his son. That was huge! Pop said to Mr. Brown he recognized that he had a skill set and certain intangibles that he did not have, in a way to reach me which Pop felt he could not and that he was big enough, to be small enough, to trust Mr. Brown in mentoring me. That was big!

Naturally, Mr. Brown said yes and took on that task and worked with me intentionally and closely for about 3.5 to 4 years. During that time he invited me to his speaking engagements, events, and seminars. He would come to Atlanta frequently and I would visit with him and sit at his feet. He dropped wisdom and knowledge on the Art of Speaking, the Art of Business and Radio, amongst other things. It was a spiritual and life clinic for me. Not only was it reaffirming, but it was also exactly what I needed at that time. My father did not have the capacity, at the time, and it gave me a greater appreciation for him and stimulated my compassion towards him and my mother.

It's hard to reach someone when a person feels like and maybe is the victim, or inherent of another's negative decisions. My parents' divorce sent me through a lot. I was placed in situations that no child should have to experience. If seeds of pain, sorrow, and resentment are not cast out, these feelings can grow and fester. And if the parent or parents don't have their seeds of possible shame or disappointment uprooted, then both can be doing life together in the garden of misunderstanding, growing in turmoil and unforgiveness, with the lack of resolve.

During my time with Mr. Brown, I not only observed his professional acumen but also how he operated as a family man. Seeing the similarities between him and my father, and how he handled them was humbling and empowering. Having these experiences with Mr. Brown caused me to see both my dad and mom differently. It was in those moments, I realized we weren't the only ones dealing with what we were dealing with. Mr. Brown was able to invoke things within me that may not have resulted from sitting with a counselor. As a result, I was more gracious.

For the parents reading this, it is sometimes difficult to connect with your children, because you gave birth to them. Much of the conflict that you are experiencing in your house with your children is because your children know the real you, not the you that is advertised. Your children know, feel and observe even though they may never say anything. Sometimes less is more. My dad recognized that he needed to do less for a season. I don't know but maybe he heard this from God. So, who is your Les? I want you to pray to God that he will lead you to someone, a mentor, facilitator, coach, and encourager. This individual should care enough about you and your child to stand in the gap.

I want to speak to every person who is like a Les Brown and can help other families that are in need, your time is now. Do it! Though you may have needs of your own or may feel like a failure or you may have certain problems in your bloodline, with your spouse, or with your children, you can still be used. My dad and I were experiencing turmoil, but the word remained the same. Luke 6:38 says, "Give and it will be given unto you, pressed down shaken together and running over should men give unto your bosom." A bosom is a place where fertility, nourishment, and growth are promoted. It's an erotic place. It's a place of new beginnings.

I am convinced that this was a result of my dad standing in the gap for so many, God sent him someone for me. Numerous people still come to me sharing the impact my dad had on their lives. He stood in the gap as a father for so many, even though he did not always feel equipped and adequate in doing so, the word still stood true. There's someone right now that needs you, give unto them and it will be given unto you. For whatever reason you have been holding back, remember there's a young person who needs your voice and gifts. There are families who need you and your support.

Les Brown, like my dad, went through things with his children, but all is well with Calvin, Ona, and the others. This blesses my heart! They're traveling the country together, speaking and standing on stages publicly, while loving on each other privately. I genuinely believe much of the reconciliation that has taken place in the Brown family is God's reward because of Les' role with the Long family. My dad specifically said to me that he wasn't afraid or intimidated by asking another man for help, as his goal was for me to become better. Don't be afraid to ask for assistance.

Ladies, you can't be a father, and men, you can't be a mother. Sometimes we have to ask for the help we need. There are fathers who are reading this book right now, who have been incarcerated; as a result, there is a struggle with connecting with your children. You want to, but there are just some words and things you don't know how to articulate just yet and your child's ear may not be ready to hear from you. Their hearts may not be open to receive from you in certain ways, because you have been gone. There are mothers who are trying to advance up the corporate ladder. You have given yourself to your career and your children feel they're not just in the back seat, but in the third row of your life, and trying to connect with them may not be an overnight thing. It's okay to invite someone else in to help and support for a certain time.

I spent the first part of my life, primarily with my mother. I only saw my dad once or twice a month and during the summer. This impacted me emotionally, psychologically, and spiritually. It can take time to repair these things or address these disconnects, so you need to find a plug. Les was the plug. Who is your plug? The plug is the catalyst of power to move. The plug serves as a connecting or reconnecting point for what was turned off.

On April 30, 2005, Les Brown stood with my family and friends at my graduation from Florida A & M University. To me, that was a very symbolic moment, because, after my graduation, my dad and I started working much more closely together. I started doing more work for the church, working with youth and things of that nature. Looking back, I see that it was not only my college graduation, but it was a graduation for us. We were being promoted and graduating out of the mess of our past, out of the miscommunication, out of the misfortunes, and everything else that was not favorable. We were graduating into a reconciled relationship.

I am forever thankful to Mr. Les Brown and even to his children for the sacrifices they made and the connection we have. When I was calling myself Young Dirty Bishop at the time, Mr. Brown would always tell me, "No son, your name is Edward; the Determined One, for there's greatness within you." It shifted so much in my life. My dad named me Edward; while helping me to see the depths of it all. Find your Les folks so that you can do more.

REFLECT NOW...PARENTS

1. Who is speaking into your children?

2. Are you comfortable with others being the village that your children will need to be successful?

3. Are you hesitant to ask for help and support in raising your seed? Why?

4. Are you dealing with insecurity?

5. Are you concerned that someone else may be more impressionable on your child than you?

REFLECT NOW...ADOLESCENTS

1. Who do you turn to for guidance aside from your parent(s)?

2. Do you feel a divine connection with a potential mentor?

3. Have you mentioned this to your parents?

4. Do you think that you can learn from a mentor while still respecting and honoring your parent(s)?

Parental Advisory

An upstanding young man listens to an explicit album that calls him or others, "Niggas." The young man is taken aback by the lyrics but understands that his peers are listening to these songs and consider them to be cool and this to be the new wave. The young man conforms to what the culture, a worldly culture, considers cool and lowers his behavior below his Kingdom standards. Over time, the lyrics, beat, and spirit of the song have made their way into the young man's heart and he begins reciting the lyrics. Since life and death are in the power of the tongue, the words the young man speaks begin to shape his life. Not only does the young man's vocabulary begin to change, but so does his behavior, image, and treatment of others.

That young man was me and many of my peers. Pop found my DMX album, *Flesh of My Flesh, Blood of My Blood,* and broke it in half, before discarding it. My dad was aware of this destructive cadence and desired to keep me on track by throwing away those tracks that would derail me! Exposure shapes one's future, both positively and negatively.

Pop was doing right in being an advised parent. He was being conscientious of what was going into my ear gates. They are called "gates" because they regulate what comes in and out of them. What goes into our ears, comes out through our mouths. Faith comes by hearing. Eve believed what she was told, although it wasn't good for her. She then told someone else what she believed. The ear is the gate to the heart. What gets into the heart is revealed by what the mouth says. Much of the music that we listen to tells us things that aren't good for us, yet the more that we listen to it, the more that it gets into our hearts, the more we believe it by learning the lyrics, and then speaking or reciting it to others.

In the chapter entitled, "Houston, We Have a Problem," I shared that my dad had used profanity towards me in the elevator after eating dinner. It wasn't until actually writing this book that I ever pondered why my dad used profanity, as I don't recall him doing it before. I never asked myself how it made me feel or how it shaped my thinking. He could have been in his feelings and that profane expression could have actually been the best way of expressing what he really wanted to do. He could have been deeply embarrassed and wanted to express to me how much my understanding meant to him.

As I reflect now, it was definitely a moment of transparency and vulnerability on his part. Again, I don't recall my dad using profanity with me, ever, except for this encounter. It showed me a different side of my dad. It reminds me of the conversation with God and Adam, everything changed when God was offended by Adam. The Word of God helps us to understand that God and Adam would have wonderful dialogue while walking together in the cool of the day. Yet, in Genesis 2, like me, Adam and Eve ate some food, and it pissed God off. Initially, God spoke calmly with them about what they had done, but when they both presented sorry and blameful excuses, God turnt up on them and all of the heritage of humanity. God didn't use profanity, but he did curse. God cursed men with the burden of having to work and till the ground. God cursed women with childbearing pains. Ever since that conversation, God's speech with humanity hasn't been the same. Was God so upset, mad, embossed, or hurt by Adam and Eve's actions, that the relationship was irreparable? Could it have been that the chastisement was actually a show of love and the curse was a measure of forgiveness?

How, you may ask? Consider the scripture that informs us that God chastens those he loves. Chasten means that God corrects and disciplines those he cares for. The text also shows us that God punishes Satan. Might this suggest that God still had a soft spot or love for the adversary? After studying this exchange between God, Adam, Eve, and Lucifer, I came to the conclusion that God was not playing any games with them when it came to obeying his commands. God's retribution was his way of getting them to understand the importance of obedience. God's curse was done in love and it was his way of demonstrating the seriousness of following his commandments. This is something that God wasn't playing about. Maybe my dad felt the same way. Maybe he was so passionate about ensuring that his son developed an understanding of managing relationships and regulating greed.

Relatability was one of my dad's strengths that attracted people to his ministry. I have a friend named Sean Demetrus Tate Senior, who once shared with me that he began following my dad's ministry after seeing him preach on his *Taking Authority* Broadcast. This program aired in jails. While incarcerated, Sean recants that my dad shared that God was working on him and his 'cussin' demon. Pop was standing in the pulpit and openly admitting that he had cursed his wife out on multiple occasions and wasn't proud of it. For Sean, this level of humanity and transparency from a preacher was nothing that he had ever seen before.

After being released from jail, he continued to study my dad and said to himself that one day he would meet my dad and share this story with him. Sean became a youth pastor, young adults' pastor and founded two churches. During his time of youth pastoring, he befriended me, and we began to establish a lifelong relationship having recorded songs together, performed on TBN (Trinity Broadcasting Network), and supported each other's families. Ultimately, two years before my dad's transition, I was able to host Sean as a guest musical artist during New Birth's main worship service. After service ended, I introduced Sean to my dad. Sean shared the story of how Pop's 'cussin' demon actually saved his life.

God truly works in mysterious ways and can use everything for anything and anything for everything. I'm in no way making excuses for my dad, but while Pop's 'cussin' demon was sinful, according to Paul's teachings (Ephesian 4:29; James 3:10), God used Pop's willingness to be transparent and honest, to help save someone who was incarcerated and put them on the path to becoming a preacher. Pop had to use those words to ensure my understanding of my wrongdoing, in a way that I could reflect on my behavior while grasping the power behind his choice to use those words.

As the Son of a Bishop, I have seen a lot of things in "church." I call it my "behind the veil" syndrome. I have seen some of your favorite preachers, pastors, televangelists, and prophetess proclaim Jesus and speak in tongue from the pulpit, but yet used a totally different tongue when 'cussin' somebody out, lying to someone, and gossiping about another immediately after leaving the pulpit. By my dad and I having that incident on the elevator, I think that I was then prepared, at a young age, to be able to feel, withstand, and cover those who I witnessed doing this. It sounds strange, but that's my revelation and I'm sticking to it. If one can see, be offended by, and cover their parents who are the closest persons to them, then one can withstand anything. Understanding my dad's 'cussin' helped me to understand God's cursing and vice-versa. Love has the ability to cover the multitude of sins according to I Peter 4:8. I take it a step further to say that it's the demonstration of love that covers...

REFLECT NOW...PARENTS

1. Do you think that it is permissible to use profanity when speaking to your children?

    a. Can it help them?

    b. Can it harm them?

2. How did your parents speak to you?

3. How did it make you feel?

4. Is there anything that you can do to change your outlook?

5. Do you desire an apology from your parents?

6. Do you think that you should apologize to your children?

REFLECT NOW...ADOLESCENTS

1. Have or do your parents use profanity when speaking to you?

2. Do they use profanity at all?

3. How does it make you feel when they use profanity while speaking to you?

4. Have you ever told them how it makes you feel?

a. Do you think that you should?

b. Do you have the courage to tell them alone or would you like someone else to be present when you speak with them?

5. How do you intend to speak to your future children?

What Kind of Son Are You?

Has anyone ever considered that maybe Noah didn't wrong his children, but instead they wronged him? They took his dignity, pride, reputation, and his good name. How is it that he raised sons (daughters) and covered them during the times when they were suffering from some less than admirable decisions that they had made, yet during Noah's time of need, most were either nowhere to be found or helped to cover him? Noah taught his sons and daughters how to be faithful. He taught them how to fully walk out the prophetic word from God, no matter what the circumstances looked like.

Noah's steadfast conviction to God's word sustained his family's life and furthermore the word and existence of humanity to this day. Had it not been for Noah being present in their lives, directing and helping them when they couldn't help themselves, they would literally be dead, and yet the best repayment they could give him was to exploit, uncover, and shame him? There are countless leaders that my dad nurtured, covered, and established that disappeared or spoke negatively about him during his time of need. As his Son, it saddens me to see those same individuals who abandoned him now try to align themselves with his legacy. I can only imagine how the children of many of our late civil rights leaders may feel to have people literally or figuratively assassinate the character of their parents, while simultaneously and publicly posturing themselves to act as if they are aligned with the predecessor. Not only is it wrong, but it is evil. It's deceptive. It's misleading. To add insult to injury, these same individuals often financially capitalized on the NIL (name, image, and likeness) of their predecessor, yet share none of the proceeds with the lineage. Jesus (Yeshua) said it best, "You did many great works in my name, but depart from me, you worker of iniquity for I never knew you." Matthew 7:21-23.

Observing my dad and how he walked with others taught me how to actually be The Word that we preach. I once heard it said that the best sermons aren't preached, but they are demonstrated in our lives. Pop demonstrated by covering people in their time of need. His covering wasn't conditional. He even covered those who attempted to uncover him. His example helped me develop the resilience to stand with my family, friends, associates and even adversaries even if they hadn't stood with me. I learned how to do unto others as I would have them do unto me. That challenge doesn't mean that others will reciprocate the gesture. It simply means that we are honoring our covenant.

If your relative (spouse, child, etc.) were to be accused of or caught in a transgression, would you disassociate yourself from them? Would you reprimand them privately and represent them publicly? Would you be polarized (frozen) and do nothing? If that same person shared with you that they were living a lifestyle or doing things that your M.E.A.L. (Morals, Ethics, Appearances, and Laws) didn't approve of, would you disown them or love them in spite of?

Young Dirty Bishop

As we embark on this next chapter, I am smiling. I'm smiling because of the great memories this topic brings to mind. In the 2000s, after college, I began to really wonder what it was like to have hands laid on you, and for those of you who attend church regularly, you know what I mean when I say laying hands on you.

I'm not talking about like in the streets when you say you're going to lay some hands, which means you were going to bust someone upside the head, come across their dome, or if you went to the party and even to the strip club, laying hands on some booty cheeks or anything like that. I mean laying of the hands for healing or restoration. This can be due to an ailment that could be physical or spiritual. I'm talking about the laying of the hands that can destroy yokes and lead to transformation. I'm talking about the laying of the hands which breaks generational curses. The laying of the hands can lead to limbs on bodies growing back, vision being repaired, and hearing being restored. I'm talking about the laying of the hands that Jesus did in the gospels and that many preachers and televangelists have both exploited and may have used improperly. I'm talking about the laying of hands where you get touched and immediately hit the floor like the Dirty Boys. I'm talking about the laying of hands which leads to the manifestation of God's wonder-working power.

You can imagine, as a pastor's offspring, I've seen the laying of hands, on multiple occasions. I grew up seeing people walk into a worship service in a wheelchair and walk out on their own two feet. I have been in conferences, with all kinds of people who couldn't see nor hear, and have their senses fully restored, but I had never seen it happen with someone I personally knew. Like many people, I was also skeptical about it. I knew that my dad was not a liar, so when I saw him lay hands on people and they fell, I believed it, but I still could not relate. For many of the people who were having hands laid on them, a lot of times they are those super, overly spiritual kinds of folks and I mean no offense, but that's just what I thought.

For someone like me, who was in church while running around these Atlanta streets, living a double life, if you will, I could not relate to a lot of those people. I recall a friend of mine, music producer Rico Love, and I discussing this intently. We became friends during his sophomore and my freshman year at Florida Agricultural & Mechanical University. He and I were remarkably similar people; alike in our thoughts and backgrounds, as he was also a pastor's kid; our aspirations, especially at that time, and so much more were similar. So here was someone that I could relate to. Rico visited with us regularly, often spending the night over my house, to wake up and go to worship service the following morning.

One Sunday, my dad called him up to the pulpit and he laid hands on him. I saw Rico go down while my dad was laying hands on him. I was in awe because, finally, there was somebody that I could relate to and I knew wouldn't go down just because. I recall asking him later, "bro, what was it like?" and I remembered him asking me, "What?" Why are you asking me? I thought you would know." I told him,

"No, just because I've been around this, doesn't mean I've experienced it. I've never gone down before." I'll never forget him saying that the only thing he could compare it to was that brief moment of peace and tranquility after having an orgasm.

I was tickled because at that time we were living a very worldly lifestyle, as I was earning my name, "Young Dirty Bishop" through promiscuous activities and he did the best he could in explaining to me what it felt like. You can imagine if someone tells you that getting hands laid on you feels post-orgasmic, you may very well become excited to get hands laid on you. It further increased my desire, if you will, into hands being laid on me. I want to caution you before you go too far in your thoughts to remember I still was a pastor's offspring and I knew a lot about church, so I wasn't going to run to every altar call just to feel this spiritual orgasm. I understood that it still needed to be an authentic thing.

Now what's funny, was that Rico was right. I had hands laid on me before, but I had never gone down or felt it. Once my dad was doing an Ishman gathering, at The Cathedral of the Holy Spirit, which was then pastored by the late Bishop Earl Paulk. Their facility was larger than our sanctuary on Snapfinger Road, as we had nearly 5,000 men to participate in the service. During that Ishman service, my dad took the time in his full bishop robe and garb, to lay hands on all of those men. This was in 1999. He touched my head, along with others, as we all walked across the pulpit and I didn't feel anything. There were other occasions where other preachers laid hands on me while speaking prophetic things over my life, yet I didn't feel anything.

In 2008, I began the journey of pastoring, by first becoming licensed and operating in the role of Youth Minister specifically over the high school and middle school ministries. At that time, I was syndicated on about sixteen stations with my radio show, *The Good Life*, in which my cousin, D'Juan Coleon Smith, was my partner. We were in about ten different cities within the southeast, including New Orleans, Jacksonville, Tampa, Macon, Augusta,

Newport News, and others. We were doing our thing. We were entertaining other opportunities for greater syndication and had just returned from a meeting with Sirius XM Satellite radio concerning programming.

I was living my dream as I was on television hosting *The Mix Master's Lounge* concert series, which was on the inspirational network, which was being taped in Charlotte. The show was in an estimated 200 million households around the world. When my dad called me after the previous Senior Director of the Youth Ministry resigned and said, "Son, I need you." Pause...I want you to understand how that hit. My dad was not the type of person to really need much. I witnessed my dad, for most of my life, being needed by people. Hell, he was even needed by me, but here I am standing around the age of 25 or 26 and my dad calls me unexpectedly and says, "Son, I need you." Once again that's him being transparent. I hit a crossroads. Here I am thinking, I'm at the tipping point of my success in entertainment and about to level up, when my dad calls me and says, "Son your church needs YOU, your family needs YOU. I need YOU. There is a calling on YOUR life."

There are a lot of people who minister the gospel would say they're called to preach and it may come through a situation like Samuel and Eli, where God called them and they heard the voice of God, or it may come through a situation where they're attracted to the glitz and glamour or the fame of ministry, but that wasn't my situation. I literally received a phone call and was called into ministry by my father. For the first six months or so, I was able to juggle being a youth minister with my entertainment endeavors, but around December of 2008, it just became too much to handle. My girlfriend, at the time, along with my partner/cousin with the radio show, both came to me and said, "Hey, this isn't working." My partner said, "Look, I think you need to focus on ministry," whereas my girlfriend and I broke up. It put a different set of challenges before me that impacted my current relationships.

If anyone doesn't know what it's like to be a youth minister, let me help you understand. It's like you're a front-line worker during a COVID-19 pandemic, which I refer to as a family's essential worker, where you are responding to families and their needs at any moment throughout the day. A student that you pastor and have built a relationship, a trustworthy relationship, will begin to share with you things they will never share with their parents in confidence. And when they have an issue in school and someone is picking on them about being lame, their clothes, their orientation, or their faith, you are the first person who comes to their minds to call, not the police, not their parents, but YOU.

When parents are having issues with their young person and can't get through to them, you're one of the first people they call before they discipline their child. When there is something in the community that's taking place and the senior pastor wants to respond to it, you're called in to strategize these initiatives. When a teen gets shot or killed, you're there for encouragement or bereavement with the family, possibly even eulogizing that individual. When the students graduate, they want you at their graduation, it may even be when they're having a party on a Saturday, which is your off day, but they want you to pull up because they love and respect you and want you to drop off $10, $15 or even $50. You literally work seven days a week! Sunday is not a day off, but a day on, because you're preaching and counseling, during and after the service. You're handling the ins and outs of actual service while leading volunteers. The same on Wednesdays (Bible Study), and on Saturdays (outreach initiatives or fundraising initiatives).

If you're a youth minister or pastor in an African American Church, you understand you probably don't have a budget and you have to create the budget in order to do the activities that everyone is expecting you to do. You have to manage social media, market the program and you have to do outreach Monday through Friday. This includes being in the community, at schools, event centers, aftercare programs, etc. in the name of God, and in the name of the ministry to push the vision forward. In my case, I was also working on a degree in divinity. You're oftentimes misunderstood by your peers, who are still in the streets or living whatever life they want to live, and you can't really do the things that you used to do. That is the case for most youth pastors. My situation was even greater because my father was the pastor of the church, so he might deal with me in ways that he would not deal with others through the familiar phrase, 'I brought you into this world and I'll take you out,' so expectations of me were completely different.

I said all of this to say, it became quite difficult for me, to honor the demands of the station that I was partnered with and to get the deliverables out in time regarding the ministry. At that time, technology was not where it is now, we were still mailing out our shows on CDs and tapes. Rendering was not as fast as it is now. It may take two or three days to render something, whereas now it only takes five or ten minutes. The processing speed was not there. Scheduling interviews was much more difficult, as there were no Zoom conference calls or podcasts. We had to be in the physical presence of those we were interviewing. I paint this picture so you can understand the challenges experienced.

As I was walking into something new, I was being stripped of something familiar. So, I stopped...I released my dreams and moved forward in youth pastoring. My ministerial license service was scheduled for February 8, 2009. I was really looking forward to this day. I invited friends and family, my mother was going to be there, my uncles were coming to town, my cousins, and my maternal grandfather. I remembered feeling like 'wow, this is pretty amazing.' One thing I did want was to have a companion by my side but at that time, I was completely single. I wasn't dating or involved with anyone. It was just me, step one, going into organized ministry. I don't think at that point I realized how many sacrifices were being made, how much I was changing, and how significant this moment would be.

During that service on Sunday afternoon, I remember my dad laying hands on all of the ministers first as we were seated for deacons being ordained, ministers being licensed, elders being ordained and then the pastors who were part of my father's fellowship, The Father's House, being commissioned. The deacons went first and then we got to the ministers, my dad chose to lay hands on all the ministers first and he saved me for last. As he called me up to the pulpit, he then acknowledged that my mom was there and thanked her, and then he asked for my bonus mother to come up and join him and he thanked her. Then he began to talk a little about some of the things he had experienced which led to the anointing on his life. He then called my uncle, James Long, who we affectionately called 'Uncle Joe' up to join him and he shared Uncle Joe's testimony. Uncle Joe had prostate cancer and so many treatments over his sixteen-year fight with cancer and it led to his body not being able to produce bone marrow. At one point and time, I believe his Prostate-Specific Antigen (PSA) numbers were over 900, he was literally on fire. Just to give you perspective, to have your levels at the number four was high and over sixteen years, cancer was not able to beat him.

He called up Uncle Joe and said he wanted him standing there, with him, because it represented a double portion for our bloodline. Then he called Elder Bernice King. She's been a dear sister to me for many years. Someone who understands much about me, because she has been down similar roads and was way ahead of me yet helped me find success in many of my struggles, as she conquered many of the same. He asked her to come to stand representing The King's bloodline and all that it embodied. I'm standing there trying to take all of this in and yes it was a lot. Even as I'm writing this now, I'm looking at what has happened over the last ten years and our connection, and simply excited about what God is going to do. Wow, the symbolism of that moment.

As Pop began to pray, he began to lay his hands on me along with my uncle and Bernice King. He then asked my mom to come up and put her hand on my shoulder along with my bonus mother. All I remember after that is floating to the floor. It was as if someone had come and picked me off my feet like Michael Jackson's 'you knock me off my feet now baby' *Off the Wall* record. If you can picture a feather, floating and seesawing, left to right as it makes its way down to the ground, is how I felt. It felt like I was being whisked away and feathered to the floor. If it was not for the pictures that I have, I probably wouldn't remember as much of that moment as I do. For the first time, regardless of how many hands were laid on me, I felt the power of the Holy Ghost and I went down like Sonny Liston or Emmanuel Pacquiao in a twelve-round battle.

As I look back, I realized where much of the power of the laying of hands comes from. It's not a one-way street where there's just a minister who touches someone, but more so a two-way street where expectation meets impartation. I didn't know it then, but the work that I was doing and what I was giving up for God was building expectation and anticipation that God will show up in a miraculous way when making sacrifices on his behalf.

Much of what I was doing in entertainment wasn't about God, it was about me. There are many people who come into a worship service with a spirit of expectation that positions them to get their healing or their sight restored. This is a direct result of expecting God to show up. They came in faith, they came knowing, they came petitioning God. They came knowing this is my only option because I've tried everything else. All the stuff I would hear my dad speak about, I was able to experience in that moment with his expectation, his testimony, and the many others who were gathered in the sanctuary. They had waited on that moment, for years, for father and son to do ministry together. That gave hope to households.

In the book of John, he records many stories and Jesus did ministry along the way and often asked people, "Do you want to be healed? Do you want to see? Do you want to hear?" Those questions were questions of anticipation. They were questions of disposition. I even ask you now as you're reading this, what do you want? Yes, God can do all things, but God is also a gentleman. He won't disrespect what is said out of our mouths but honor the true intentions of the desires of our hearts, Jesus says, 'Whatever you ask in my name, you can have.' Often, we ask him things with our mouths that our whole being isn't yet yearning for or ready to receive.

I stand here as a brother, to say to you that there is true power in the laying on of the hands. Have you ever been skeptical? It's okay to say yes, as have I. But being one that is like you, we were just like the disciple Thomas, who was a doubter, and we needed a true touch. I've gotten my touch and now I can share with you that it's true and it came through working...the works of our father coupled with developing a true need for his kingdom and true expectation.

I challenge you to develop in all three of those areas. God didn't do stuff just for our fancy, he does stuff for a divine purpose. I was convicted and realized my anointing at the same time. I was convicted to stop being Young Dirty, living a promiscuous lifestyle, and recognized the anointing I had in that moment to go forward representing the change agent for my bloodline, for social changes in my African American heritage, and ultimately for God's kingdom. Even as I'm writing this, I'm becoming clearer about it. God can't waste a hand. It's too tough to find good hands to waste it on impure intentions.

We understand the intentions that God has for us, it helps us to understand what we're carrying and who we're carrying it for. My family has been through a lot and yours probably has too. When my dad said he needed his brother, my uncle, to stand with him because of what I was called to do, he needed a double portion. In meekness, you may say, 'What is my portion?' 'I don't know my father.' 'I don't know my uncle.' 'My uncles don't care about me.' 'My aunts don't care about me.' I push you to go back to those three things and cry out to God. Remember God grants his promises; however, it is sometimes contingent on you, your beliefs, and your expectations. Say, "Lord, I need you and your anointing on my life because I have to break this cycle in my family. I have to break this curse over my family. This is the challenge that's been uniquely extended to me that you knew before the foundation of the earth. I not only recognize this, but I am also humble enough to say, I can't do it without your touch Lord."

Take a moment on these lines here. Write down what kind of touch you need from God. What areas do you need him to touch? Where do you need your confidence to increase? Where do you need your faith increased? What are you expecting God to do for you now? Next year? Believe in God for all things. He is exactly who you believe him to be.

The words my dad said were true, that I would need a double portion because after laying hands on me, in February of 2008, my dad thought he would live forever, and in less than ten years, he's no longer here on earth. Not only is my dad gone, but my uncle passed away three years after that. I received a double portion from my father and my uncle. Lord knows I could use their wisdom now, but they gave it to me there. They gave me the strength to conquer cancer, the strength to stand against adversity, the strength to win, the strength to live, and the strength to not conform. My Uncle Joe was also a pastor in Florida. They equipped me then and now with the strength to be a minister and rightly divide the word even in their physical absence. Tell God what you need and expect that you will receive it.

I'll close with something to make you laugh. Later that night after we had the banquet, and concluded the celebrations after the service, my dad pulled me to the side and said, "God gave me that power tonight, didn't he?" I said, "Yeah, what you mean?" He said, "You noticed your mom went down too?" I went back and watched the tapes and got the pictures. I saw my mom in the background laid out on the floor with her legs twisted around like the witch of the east underneath the house in Kansas in the *Wizard of Oz*. On the video, she went down before I did. So that double portion power flowed through me to her and I pray it has helped her life to be everything that it's supposed to be. Like I said, the power in the laying of the hands is true, so let it work on your behalf.

What have you been anointed to do? Are you trying to do things in your own strength or are you allowing the perfect process of God to prepare you for the purpose of your life? Do you want the anointing for self-glory or God's glory? Have you anointed your family, your children, your spouse, your workplace, your business, your home, or your vehicle(s)?

Bernice King

Vanessa Long & Pastor James "Joe" Long

Deacon Lewis Houston

The Burden of the Building

As I'm writing this chapter today, it is amazing to see what is taking place in these pseudo-United States and around the world. When we set out to write this book, I did some deep thinking and brainstorming on the discussions that my dad and I had, which ones I felt would be timely for now and which ones I felt were most transparent, yet impactful, but be easily understood by a multitude of people. This chapter, of course, is on one of those topics that I felt met all of that criteria and now having come to the point of writing it, I am clear it does because of our current reality. Right now, we are dealing with the Coronavirus aka COVID-19, along with protests happening in all 50 states and now other countries as a result of the murder of George Floyd.

When my father was selected by the deacon board and board of trustees to pastor New Birth Missionary Baptist Church in 1987, the church had just relocated to 2778 Snapfinger Road, Decatur, Georgia 30034, from Scottsdale, Georgia where the church split had taken place. My older sibling Eric and I came to the church at the same time as my father. When we became a part of New Birth, it was a 300-member congregation, holding services in a 150-seat sanctuary. Over the next three years, the ministry grew from that number to about 8,000 members which literally had the church bursting at the seams from a physical space standpoint, creating a need for more space. So, my father led the planning to build a new sanctuary next door on the same property that held 2,000 people.

From there, growth continued. A few short years later, we had to install a 1,500-seat balcony within that 2,000-seat sanctuary bringing the capacity of this new sanctuary to 3,500. We remained in this facility for about seven years, but continued growing, leading to (yet again) the need for a larger building. Prior to building a new facility, Pop explored many other creative options to be able to have all the members under one roof, simultaneously.

We began holding Resurrection services at the Georgia Dome, which became the largest Resurrection Sunday gathering in the world. It even eclipsed gatherings at the Vatican with more than 30,000 people attending annually. We would also hold our New Year's watch night services at the Georgia Dome. We hosted the largest watch night faith-based New Year's gathering. Additionally, we would have impromptu unity services that were held at Philips Arena in downtown Atlanta. We would have special services for both respective genders in our congregation. This led to Pop hosting Bishop T.D. Jakes' Manpower conferences. But none of these creative measures lead to sustainability for the traditional Sunday audience. As you could imagine, preaching three services each Sunday from roughly 6:00 am to 3:00 pm can begin to take a toll on anyone.

Pop led New Birth once again into another real estate venture. As we sold some land that was previously acquired and leveraged, we used that to purchase land in Lithonia, Georgia, which is now Stonecrest and home to the present edifice of New Birth. On this land, Pop had a vision for a lot of things including athletic fields, a family life center (inclusive of basketball courts, fitness center), state of the art industrial kitchen, cafeteria for serving school students, and an event space to host community events. A food bank and cafeteria to serve those in need, pool, ratchet ball facilities, prayer walks and trails, an amphitheater, large sanctuary, chapel, bookstore, cafe, transitional housing, gardening, and multipurpose green space for activities. Also, many entrances to the property include a dedicated exit to an industrial highway, a grade school, a biblical institute, and many other facilities and auxiliaries to provide an array of services.

One day, while having a staff meeting, Pop shared the vision God had given him. He shared that we would make this transition in phases from the present location of the church, going into the family life center which would be completed first in phase one, moving into the sanctuary during phase two, and then the other auxiliaries would be completed in phase three. He then said something profound. He said God told him we would not go and could not go into the sanctuary until it was paid off and we were debt-free. That's a big statement to make while building a multimillion-dollar campus. This project would cost tens of million dollars, but my father was clear that was what God shared with him. If you know anything about my dad, you know he was serious about what God said.

Afterward, he shared this same vision, for the new facility, with the other auxiliaries of the church and ultimately with the membership. You can imagine it created quite a frenzy. Everyone was excited and ready to play their part in this historical move. In 1999, we loaded up some Kingsmen Coach buses on an early Saturday morning, with as many members as we could. We loaded about 20 buses and the rest went in their cars. We had a motorcade that would've put the wedding day train of any queen to shame. We drove from the previous New Birth on Snapfinger Road to the new property at 6400 Woodrow Road, now known as Bishop Eddie Lee Long Parkway in Stonecrest, Georgia. We were able to drive out to this property and look around and see the vision, pray and prophesy over our new beginnings. After that, the work began, we broke ground on the family life center.

After its completion in 2000, we began holding worship services there. We sold the property at 2778 Snapfinger Road to Ray of Hope Christian Church which is pastored by our sister, Dr. Cynthia Hale. While at the new property, we held multiple services on Sundays in the family life center. We erected a stage and put down nearly 4,000 chairs on the basketball court floor. We held services in the gymnasium, now known as the Bishop Eddie Lee Long Family Life Center, for nearly two years. Though we were in a gym, it felt like we were in the Sistine Chapel come Sunday morning. We occupied every space. The auxiliary spaces we had in this new facility were less than the old facility, yet we maximized every inch of it, and our operations were executed like clockwork.

Sporadically, my dad would make mention to associates of what God said to him about not moving into the new sanctuary until it was paid off and we were debt-free. At the time, I don't think he knew the significance of what he was saying. Paul reminds us that we can only prophesy in part. But he knew that what he was saying was significant and would have an impact on future generations.

Lo and behold, as time went on, the new sanctuary was completed around February 2001, which was my senior year in high school. Now both buildings mean a great deal to me. My high school graduation was held at New Birth on June 1, 2001, and it was the first graduation to be held in the building. My dad coordinated the efforts to build the buildings. He leveraged political and governmental relationships to get various things approved, such as permits and zoning. Yet, while he was working that angle, I too was working literally building the buildings. I worked to help construct the first building, which was the family life center under the direction of Joseph Washington and Integrity Construction, running the bulldozer, cleaning debris off the grounds, and loading it into dumpsters and onto dump trucks to be hauled away. During this time, I also learned how to read blueprints and was exposed to the process of excavation, while being a junior in high school. I was also taking a drafting class concerning architecture.

When we began working on the main sanctuary, I worked under the direction of Warren Miller and Miller Enterprises, where we were installing the fiber optic system into the facility. I never knew what fiber optics were before. This experience allowed me the opportunity to run wiring throughout the entire building. To this day, while most people walk in and see the marble floors, carpet, tile, sheetrock walls, crown molding, drop ceilings, art on the walls, statues, seats, pews, a stage, or screen, I see the building inside out and from a structural standpoint because of the hands-on role I was commissioned to play.

At some point in this faithful process, my dad decided to do what he had been told not to do, which was to move into the building even though it wasn't paid off. He was still human and I'm sure at some point he felt overwhelmed, due to the ongoing assessments, contract agreements, and individuals wanting to move into the building against what he was told. Knowing him, his commitment, the price, knowing the pride he took in his word, this was not an easy decision for him to make. Yet a decision was made, and we moved into the new sanctuary holding the first service in March of 2001.

What's ironic is that we moved from Snapfinger Road to Woodrow Road to create more space and to relieve some of the burdens he was carrying. But, moving into the new building before God said to move only created a bigger burden - millions in a mortgage. However, the burden, I mean the building, was still a blessing. The new sanctuary held just less than 7,000 people, with 500 in the chapel, and 4,000 that could still fit in the family life center. You could see roughly 11,000 people in one setting. These were high times for New Birth with multiple services and a brand-new state-of-the-art building on more than 240 acres of land. All of that was accompanied with a new and outstanding price tag, which ultimately shifted the ministry.

My father and the ministry realized why God told him not to go into the building without it being paid off. The increased mortgage line item would now impact overall funds which were allocated strictly for ministry. Much of these funds would have to be reappropriated and no longer used for ministry, but now be used to service the mortgage. If you've ever purchased a house and received a significant loan, you understand the interest you pay is pretty significant in comparison to the principal amount that you financed. Had we faithfully raised the money to take care of the principal, we wouldn't have faced much of the debt that the ministry came to face.

Now I do want to point out that most churches around the world have a mortgage, which means they have debt. This is not an abnormal thing, and it's not necessarily a bad thing. However, in my father's case, God was doing a new thing in challenging his faith and the faith of our local church to do something in a new way. We had to trust God and be committed to God in the process so that God could do something at New Birth that could reverberate to every other ministry. This experience could serve as a blueprint to how to go into a state-of-the-art edifice while being debt-free. I know this is something that God desired to see and because he is no respecter of persons, he will move here and there, until He identifies someone who He can work through to accomplish what He is looking to do.

I was so encouraged some time ago when I heard Pastor Mike Todd tell the story of how he and the Transformation Church family acquired and moved into a multimillion-dollar facility, debt-free, simply because he chose to listen to God. Many pastors are now calling him, to sit at his feet, to understand how it is that he was able to do that in this day and time.

While in Miami, Florida, in 2012, I had the opportunity to be in the room with Bishop Victor

Curry, the legendary Reverend Jasper Williams, Jr., and my father. They were sharing stories about obstacles they overcame in ministry, as well as their future goals. Bishop Curry was facilitating a service to honor Pop and invited Pastor Williams to be the guest speaker. During this time, our family was still working through the tension of the various lawsuits filed against my dad. In light of these allegations many preachers had stopped supporting my dad, but Mr. Hoopology himself, Reverend Jasper Williams, Jr. felt it his duty to publicly preach a sermon of edification and honor concerning Pop.

During their conversation, my dad said something key. Pop said that he just wanted to get the debt off the building, and he didn't want me to have to deal with that. Pastor Williams cosigned the statement. Pastor Williams and The Salem Bible Church had recently built a new facility in Lithonia, Georgia and his son, Joseph Williams, was pastor. This was the first freakin' time that I had ever heard my dad say a definitive statement concerning me and succession. I'm sitting there like what!!! My mind instantly began recanting the many conversations that we'd had, where he told my siblings and I that he didn't want us to pastor the church. He cajoled us to explore other things and seek God for ourselves. I never thought that he really felt like that. I always felt he was deflecting or trying to distract us from pursuing ministry for reasons I couldn't place my finger on it at the time. You must understand that anytime my dad and I discussed the church, beyond me running from ministry in my early years, he would say to me that he wouldn't wish any of what he had to endure while pastoring New Birth onto any of his children. He would tell me to consider other things and had publicly and privately positioned his other spiritual sons and in-house ministers like Pastor Jesse Curney, Bishop Terrell Murphy, and Pastor Charles Jenkins to be his successors.

From about 2012, until the time of Pop's transition, I had become more focused on ministry which led to him utilizing me not only as a youth pastor but also as a leader in the sanctuary which led to me preaching more in house, especially during the months leading up to his transition. Many members have told me that this gave them the impression I was being groomed to be his successor. As if I wasn't already flabbergasted enough, my dad made another gut-busting statement within the conversation with Bishop Curry and Pastor Williams. He shared that if he could do it all again, he would have never built the building, as it changed so much. That was my first-time hearing that as well, but it was a statement that I would hear him echo to many others as time went on. It was a huge statement that so much was wrapped up in. He was acknowledging how heavy it was to carry the ministry to the point where it felt like a burden. God's original intent was for it to be a blessing, but the burden that he was feeling, through his love for me (us), he did not want to impart on me or any of his children.

I was very appreciative of Bishop Curry and Pastor Williams for their outpour of love for my dad. Their actions were teaching me a lesson of how to stand with my friends in troubled times. I'm thankful that they allowed me to be in the room. They showed me how to be open in private amongst friends while building the strength to be transparent in public. This conversation was surreal to me. I'm sitting in the audience of three of the most transformational spiritual leaders as they trade war stories and triumphant testimonies. On one hand, I'm seeing the agape love being demonstrated while gleaning from the sermons of their collective lives. On the other hand, I'm relishing in the astonishment of the revelations that my dad shared concerning me and the church building.

New Birth's sanctuary is a beautiful edifice. People literally travel from around the world to see it. I've seen many pastors and world leaders come from all around the world just to sit at my father's feet and gain wisdom and insight on how he built it. One might even consider the church as one of the mighty wonders of the world. Isn't that a tough position to be in, for people to be celebrating something that you wished you had never done? It's a tough place to be grieved by something that excites everyone else. I'm talking to pastors now that have received a word from God about something to do or not to do, but they're feeling pressure from the board, constituents, congregation, family members, their spouse, or children. All of these significant people want you to do something contrary to what you know God spoke to you about. Being a leader is not easy. I am not sharing this story to defame or devalue my father. Great leaders do great exploits but also have great struggles. Overcoming these struggles is what creates greatness. That's why we all need The Holy Spirit.

Moses was able to hold a snake as a staff in combination. He was able to lead multitudes out of the Egyptian empire. He was able to speak to water and it parted. Moses was able to script our foundational principles into rock and stone, yet he also fell short because of his temperament. David was able to win many wars, build a city, unite kingdoms, yet he struggled with sexual fidelity and fatherhood.

To every leader, not just pastors, but leaders of the household, an organization, a team, I'm speaking and writing to you. I'm even writing to myself. Do what God tells you to do. The decisions that we make, or don't make, will impact our families. They will impact those we lead, command, and serve.

For us, the finances of our ministry and the attention needed played a major role in succession. My dad said something else about the building. Around 2014, churches across the country were beginning to host fewer people in their pews, as the culture began to shift. People were beginning to stream as others were taking less interest in church. My dad said there will come a time when all these buildings we have built won't even matter. I go back to my opening statement of this chapter; it seems like we have come to that place. Many jurisdictions are locked down, most churches are closed, people are struggling with standing next to one another, and are advised to give one another six feet. This is four years after his transition, and no real ministry is being done at the building. Ministry is taking place digitally or through delivery; however, the financial obligations to the building must still be paid, even on those that are not being used.

In 1999, when God spoke to my dad, he shared what God said. He wasn't crazy, he was more than prophetic and had heard from God clearly. Now more than 20 years later, we're seeing why God said what he said. He had radical faith to say it while his own team members were thinking, this man is crazy. To build a building and let it sit unoccupied until it's paid for just doesn't make sense to man. But the instructions didn't come from man, they came from God.

Noah built a building, an ark, at the command of God and then it had to sit inoperable, until an appointed time. Our ministry started off as a movement, because we were in the streets heavily, marching, doing missionary work, going door to door, feeding the needy, impacting schools, fully entrenched in the community. Sometimes what stops movements are the cost of monuments. If Pop could have done it again, I don't think that he would not have built the building, but I do think he would have waited until it was paid off, before occupying the space. It pains my heart to know that the decision concerning succession came down to finances. Succession should come as a directive of God. Mantles should be passed, and the passing of mantles should be led by the Holy Spirit.

Not too long after my dad transitioned, I had conversations with two of his counterparts. The first was with Bishop Carl Smith of New Destiny Church (formerly New Birth California). After years of successfully pastoring the church and building a large ministry, he felt God instructed him to submit the ministry under my father's tutelage and become part of the New Birth Church Association. He did and served faithfully for more than a decade. Bishop Carl Smith visited my dad at his home about two months before he passed. I had been staying at my dad's house and helping to care for him while he was believing God to be healed from the pancreatic cancer diagnosis. I wasn't at the house at the time Bishop Smith visited. Although it was uncharacteristic of me, I left without making the bed. I must have been rushing. Bishop Smith shared with me that he and my dad walked throughout the house talking, planning, reminiscing, and the likes when they came to the room that I was sleeping in. They had somehow begun to discuss me. While doing so, my dad pointed out that I had left without making the bed and made a joke of it knowing how neat I am. What he shared next was most impactful to me.

Bishop Smith told me that my dad said to him, "At the end of the day I'd love to see the church go to EDward." Unbeknownst to me, but once again Pop was being transparent with someone concerning me and the future of the church. I took what Bishop Smith shared with me as confirmation of the thoughts I had developed and suppressed over the years. I had come to the resolution that my dad was simply concerned for and a bit scared to place me in the role of senior pastor. Any good father wants to protect their children from pain, scrutiny, turmoil, public opinion, betrayal and more. He knew what he had endured in building a kingdom embassy, an outspoken ministry, so he knew what came with it. Considering a spiritual son would still perpetuate the same message of the house and it is easier to see one who is like your son being challenged versus your own flesh and blood.

If his words to Bishop Smith weren't enough consolation, they were shared with me by another one of his associates. Bishop George Bloomer, Bishop Phillip Thomas, and I were on a conference call together where Bishop Bloomer was coaching me on some things concerning my future in ministry. While on the call, Bishop Bloomer turned a corner and began sharing with me how he and my dad had a conversation concerning me, where my dad told him he wanted me to be his successor and he just felt that I needed more time and coaching. Wow! Here it was once again, I was hearing my dad's desire being reverberated. The same heart was being echoed nearly verbatim out of the mouths of two bishops who didn't know each other, coupled with what I heard my dad say years prior.

After my dad's transition, my desires and hope were that the church would have placed a team of counselors around me, to prepare and groom me for the role, if they believed I wasn't ready. When King David passed, Solomon was young and had not spent much time with his father, yet a team of counselors trained and advised him, which led to him being known as one of the wisest and richest men to ever live. The power of a plan, coupled with the alignment of kingdom principles, can accomplish the miraculous. An understanding of church and its operations, versus Kingdom and legacy, are two different things. My dad preached Kingdom. We understood Kingdom. He desired Kingdom.

As one who is preparing to be a father, I empathize with my father's plight. I'm preparing to have my first offspring and beginning to understand the responsibility of fatherhood. I once shared with him that I am a souldier (a soldier in God's Kingdom that fights for souls) and challenged him not to shelter me from the fight. I said, "Pop, you've trained me for war, why not let me fight?" I'm understanding his why.

Since Pop's transition, I have been asked the question at least a billion times, "Why didn't your dad name you his successor?" It's a question that I have come to expect. Well, for those who want to know why, that's the best "why" that I have! My goal has not been to answer the question for my father but rather to continue doing the Kingdom works and showing the unconditional love of God to all. I have been trained and feel convicted to do so. I understand that what is in me, can be manifested anywhere, in buildings and outside of the four walls.

My great concern is also that the congregants and the community, be served and the kingdom message and sound that is the fabric of that church, be perpetuated. I remain connected to the community, serving as a police chaplain for the local police department, chaplain for the Stephenson High School football team, a program manager for youth, and an intrapreneur. Additionally, I serve in multiple capacities with various educational programs, intergenerational food and security programs, while still providing pastoral care through bereavement, counseling, officiating weddings, baptisms, and christenings. Also bringing awareness and solutions to community issues through media platforms like radio and television broadcasts.

Naturally, my desire was to continue our familial legacy at our home church. To hear the desires of my dad reverberated to me two times over serves as confirmation. It validates what others question. It fortifies what others object to. It authenticates what others emulate. What's in my father was bigger than a building, yet the pain that he endured was beyond impressionable. God so loved the world that He gave His only begotten son. It just so happens that my dad loved his son so, that he wanted to protect his son from this world.

REFLECT NOW...

1. What is your business?

2. Is your family involved in it? If not, how can they be?

3. Do you have a succession plan for your family?

4. Have you communicated this plan with them?

5. Are you open to receiving their commentary and opinions?

6. Have you talked to your parents about your roles in their endeavors?

7. Are you willing to work with them to achieve a common goal?

8. What has God instructed you to do concerning your family?

9. Have you considered what the impact of obedience or disobedience will be on your family?

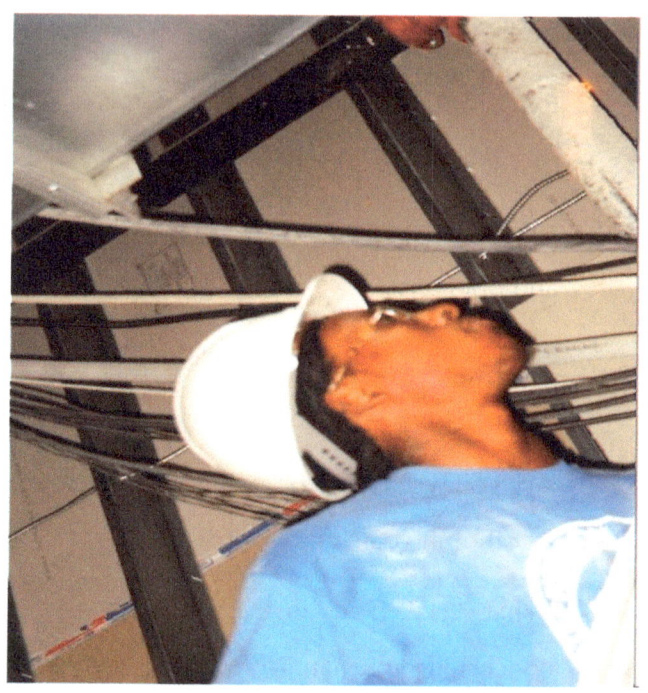

People Are People

Over time, New Birth was beginning to be known as the celebrity church. It was nothing to come to a Sunday morning worship service and see a celebrity seated beside you. This was both unintentional and intentional. It was unintentional in the sense that what Pop was preaching, what was coming out of his mouth and spirit, was so magnetic, it caused people to seek him and gravitate to him. He was preaching a kingdom message which had never been heard in this manner.

Pop wasn't a hooper. He never developed that hooping sensational craft. He was just who he was and preached how he preached. He developed into something that had never existed before. He was an orator, a storyteller, and was very charismatic, but more importantly, he genuinely loved people and shared the word in a way people could understand. The same love he showed to the unknown lay member that was on the last row in the church, was the same love he showed to many of the influencers and celebrities that came to the church.

Nowadays, we see ministers who literally target certain celebrities to try to build a relationship with them to use them, their resources, money, etc. but that's not what my dad did. He was intentional in loving all people. It was what influencers were looking for to cause them to open up and love him back. It's incredibly sad to see, but it's true that now we're in an age where many pastors are clout chasers. They are specifically targeting certain people (i.e., celebrities, influencers, and athletes), for the sole purpose of building their brand and capitalizing off of those people's resources. Giving more attention to what those people can do for them and their church ministry, rather than what they as a minister can do for the soul of that person. It breaks my heart to see this and it's not something I can cosign. You see many of the pastors that do this will be the main ones to say they don't. But the truth of the matter is, we can tell because of the spirit it's done in. Words across the microphone are just words, but you can tell when someone really cares about you by the love they show you.

Some of the relationships Pop had were no mystery. One of the most prolific performers of our time became like a brother to me, and that person was Usher Raymond. Usher and my dad developed a close relationship to the point where Usher referred to my dad as dad. Pop intentionally mentored him at a critical time in his life. Pop never asked him to get on the microphone when he came to church because that was not the point of him being there. His point of being at church was the same reason everyone else was there, to have an authentic encounter with Christ and be equipped to manage the happenings of his life.

Pop also worked very closely with Shad Moss aka Bow Wow. I remembered when he and Bow Wow considered exchanging cars. Bow Wow came to the church in his yellow Lambo and Pop was just so tickled by it. He wanted to sit in it. A few of us gathered in the garage of the church and Bow Wow told him, "Dad just hop in." It took Pop about three or four minutes to get into the car because he was too big for it. Pop did not like tight spaces. He would get claustrophobic and start panicking. While sitting in the car for a few minutes, he smiled, took his picture, and he got the HELLO out of that car.

I remember when I first met Ciara at the church. After her initial visit, she became a regular attendee. Again, it was the kingdom that he embodied, and it was love that spewed out of him that was magnetic. It's funny because at that time, she had just dropped 'Goodies' and I had the biggest crush on her. He once invited her to come by the house just to hang out with our family. I didn't know what to do when he told me that. I was beyond excited and had to get myself together because Ciara was coming by the house.

Other artists like Michelle Williams, Kirk Franklin, Deion Sanders, Montell Jordan, Tye Tribett, Israel Haughton and so many others, really took to Pop as a mentor and a father figure in their life. Some artists didn't develop as close of a relationship but did call upon him for counsel and guidance at certain points within their lives and not necessarily because something negative was happening. Many simply had opportunities arise and they wanted to find favor in what they were pursuing. I remember Sean "Diddy" Combs coming by the former New Birth building and meeting with Pop concerning some upcoming things in his life. Others that visited included Missy Elliott and Beyoncé while she was filming *The Fighting Temptations*. Yeah ladies, I met "B."

One of the most endearing relationships he fostered was with Lisa "Left Eye" Lopes. She was misunderstood by many people, as she had many public experiences concerning her dating relationships, her group, and more. Yet, Pop understood Lisa and when she tragically transitioned, it really broke his heart. He hosted her homegoing at New Birth. While it was a spectacle to many, as all of Atlanta's Black Hollywood was in attendance, I watched him really struggle during that season. He continued to walk with the family for quite a while after that, covering them and making sure they had what they needed.

Under Pop's leadership, New Birth was not just a place that attracted celebrities and influencers, but it was a place that produced notable influencers and kingdom ambassadors. People like William Murphy, Darwin Hobbs, Sam Collier, Byron Cage, Dottie Peoples, John Gray, and many others who served in the house under Pop's tutelage and co-labored with him went on to lead impactful faith careers. The legendary group, Jagged Edge, was formed at New Birth. Kyle Norman's father and uncle were two of the founding deacons of the church. Brandon and Brian Casey's mother was one of the worship leaders of the church. Growing up, being exposed to and working with high profile individuals, slowly became my new normal, but it wasn't necessarily easy. I remember the situation which shifted me from being caught up in celebrity and stardom, to accepting the celebrity and stars' humanity.

When I was nineteen, while enrolled at Florida A & M University, I was on the radio in Tallahassee and I had my own Friday afternoon drive time Hip-Hop show. On one particular Sunday, while I was back in

Atlanta, Georgia visiting, I was asked to escort a certain celebrity to my dad's office after the service. While escorting them to the office, we made a bit of small talk and they seemed to be rather approachable. I shared with them that I had a radio show and that I would love to get a radio drop from them for my show. At that time, phones did not have the recording option, so I used to keep a small mini recording device with me at all times.

The artist's response to me was, 'No, I don't want to do it.' Honestly, I was taken aback. As we continued to walk to the entrance of my dad's office, the artist greeted my dad with major excitement and after things settled down, my dad then introduced me and said, "Hey, you know this is my son." The artist said, "Oh, I did not know that." Then they said to me, "I don't mind doing that drop for you if you still want it." At that moment, I was good on the artist. This artist wasn't a mainstream artist, but was a Christian artist, which meant being in church was not foreign to them. This was their norm. It really bothered me to see the fakeness if you will. Me being stubborn, I let it ride and said I was cool without getting the drop.

Later that evening when we were at the house, I thanked my dad for introducing me to the artist, and then I gave him the back story and told him how it made me feel. At that moment, Pop taught me one of the biggest lessons ever, as a music artist, radio personality, minister, and all the other things I embody. It still rings true and has a direct impact on my present career. The lesson that he taught me, I haven't and will never forget. For anyone pursuing a career in the entertainment business, this lesson should be committed to memory and included in Donald Passman's book entitled, *All You Need to Know About the Music Business*. He shared a powerful message that should be applied to anyone connected to the industry, regardless of their position or level of notoriety.

My dad looked at me and he said, "I'm glad that happened because now you should understand that *People Are People*. I have watched you somewhat get caught up in the celebrity and hype, and I didn't know how to say this to you but, people are people. Those folks that you are excited about are no different than you. Yet most of them have way more issues than you can ever imagine and they're one step away from losing their minds." It totally revolutionized my outlook on everything concerning entertainment. I have never been the fanatical type of person, yet at the same time, I was a fan of a lot of people, and I have to say like anyone else, I put certain people on pedestals. At that moment, I knocked all the pedestals down. I took down artist posters from my wall after hearing my dad preach about the significance of posters and pictures posted in our houses. In the message, he pointed out that whatever we hang on our walls serves as demi-gods or idols. We have to be careful as to what we hang on our walls because the image of that person or persons, we are now allowing into our house, and the word of the Lord says, 'as for me and my house, we will serve the Lord.'

I can do a whole message on that right now. Even about what we watch and bring in our house through the television and radio, but that's not what I'm talking about right now. I took down posters and totally revamped my approach to artists and it helped me to understand the impact my dad was having on various people's lives. Not everyone that he was working with was 'in a bad state'. But 'people are people' was a blanket statement to say that the only difference between me and them was that they just had a bigger platform which meant that their gifts and talents were amplified for more people to see and more people to celebrate. But in the same breath, so were their shortcomings, personal problems, and issues.

It's such a compassionate statement. It challenged my thinking, and it should challenge yours, to hold people accountable for who they are, opposed to who people see them as, or think they are because of their celebrity. Jesus was not a respecter of persons and knowing the gifts God gave us does not prevent our individual struggles. Some of the issues, struggles, problems, or needs that some of these celebrities have, I was exposed to and

I learned then how not to exploit them and run and tell my friends what they were dealing with. I learned early how to cover, pray, and create a safe place for them to share what they're going through and not worry about it coming back on them negatively. Do you think that you have that covering ability? It's God's grace. I learned the grace of God through the many teachings of my father. Paul says that "grace covers." We also understand according to 1 Peter 4:8, "Love covers a multitude of sins."

Until this day, when I hear about artists dealing or struggling with different things, I cover them and bridle my tongue. Whether it be drugs or promiscuity, money embezzlement, tax evasion, family issues, divorce, or anything else, I cover. I don't run to my social media account to put this artist down because I understand that people are people and to whom much is given, much is required. If you're reading this, and you've never had much, you really don't know how you would respond if you were given much. If you were given the opportunity to have sex with a different person every night because people were throwing themselves at you, would you be able to handle that 'much' which was given to you? If you were given access to things that you can only dream about right now, would your character allow you to still make the decisions based on what's right as opposed to your weakness?

His statement convicted me when I was nineteen years old concerning that faith-based superstar who initially refused me by telling me no. They declined doing the radio drop but adjusted after finding out I was Bishop Long's son. Celebrities are also looking for celebrities and they clout chase as well because they're people. I had to realize that I too was attempting to capitalize off this celebrity as well. Even though this artist was a faith-based artist, who was at church, the place where their primary income came from, at that moment, they did not want to have to be a celebrity or have to work. Maybe I wasn't respecting the sanctity of that moment. They may have heard a word from God which was taking root in them and needed that moment of solitude away from the celebrity, to be just what Pop said, a person. Not a rock star, not a brand, but just a person.

I learned you must be sensitive and not be offended by others' needs. I learned that sometimes it's just about being in the present. There may be no picture to show. I may not get a drop to play on my radio show to prove I met an individual comfortable with cosigning my movement. There may be none of that to publicly broadcast where I'm leveraging that person's celebrity to be a blessing to what I'm doing. Maybe I should just be a blessing to them by allowing them a moment to let their hair down and be a person.

When I took my pastoral care classes, one of the first things I learned from Dr. Monty Norwood of Beulah Heights University was the ministry of presence. When people are dealing with trauma and we do visits at their home, hospital, or an alternate location, we don't go in and ask a bunch of questions. We go in and simply comfort them by saying, 'I'm here. You don't have to talk if you don't want to or you can if you so desire. I'm just going to sit here with you to provide comfort through my presence.' It's the ministry of presence that somebody of God is there to help a person feel the presence of God by providing the comfort that things will be alright. Through that lesson, I stopped being a fan of anyone. Instead of viewing people as celebrities, I just chose the root word of celebrity which is celebrate. Like my dad, I just chose to be unintentionally intentional in celebrating everyone.

Now as I move around, it does not matter if a person is world renown or a person who sits on the last pew in the sanctuary, that no one knows, my intent is to love everyone just as Jesus did because now, I understand, thanks to my dad teaching me, "people are people."

REFLECT NOW:

1. Who are you idolizing?

2. Why do you revere them?

3. Does this have a positive or negative effect on how you feel about yourself?

4. Do you have the same or higher reverence for God, your loved ones, and/or yourself?

5. What can you do to celebrate others without idolizing them?

Sean "Puff Daddy – P. Diddy" Combs

Shad "Bow Wow" Moss

Sha'reef De La Cruz, Rico Love, & Ciara Harris

Usher Raymond

Kirk Franklin

Deion Sanders & Rico Love

One More Rep

Pop was the gladiator preacher. He was the Hulk Hogan of ministry, the Mr. T of the faith, and the Mike Tyson of The Kingdom. He wore muscle shirts under priest robes that glorified his biceps, triceps, and veiny forearms. Everything about his physique embodied and exemplified the kingdom. Many preachers to this day still aim to emulate his stature, attire, swag, inflections, word usage, and demeanor. But what he exhibited on the outside was just an authentic reflection of who he was on the inside. He had a win, dominate, lead the way, champion the day, kingdom mindset.

When he became sick with cancer, he began to lose weight and muscle mass at a very rapid pace. In a matter of five months, he went from weighing roughly 240 pounds to 140 pounds. You can imagine that this would be met with various insecurities for anyone. Though he struggled with his image, he didn't let himself get down about it.

New Birth was one of the first churches to ever have a fitness center because Pop believed it was necessary to not only exercise our spirit but to also steward our temple or physical. Like the Gladiator King David, Pop also deemed it important to demonstrate to his followers how to actively take care of the temple. For this reason, even though we had a full gym at the house, he would still go to the Sampson Health & Fitness Center at the Bishop Eddie L. Long Family Life Center and work out with the members. This made what he exemplified, obtainable to everyone.

I remember one day in August of 2016 when he came to me and said let's go downstairs and workout. Now I have always been athletic, yet slim. I played football, basketball, and ran track, yet I have always been tall, fit, and slim. My stature and image come from my grandfather, Reverend Floyd Long, II. At this time, Pop was slimmer than me, but we went to the gym and did a full workout. On our first set we agreed to do ten, he went first. When he got to ten, he did one more which made eleven. Naturally, I said," You know we were only doing ten." He looked and said, "I always do one extra." He continued to say, during the time that he was being sued, he realized he was going to have to develop the habit of going the extra mile, and since then he always did one extra rep. Wow! That hit! It mentally prepared him for the course ahead.

My high school football defensive back and track coach, Donald Sellers, would tell us not to run to the line but to run through the line. To run to the line means that you can stop when you get there, which ultimately means that you let up before you got to the goal. Letting up slows us down, giving the enemy room to catch up, causing it to take a little longer before you get to the goal and shift us from the head of the pack to the middle of the pack and more. Don't coast through life. Running through the line means we are going to have to take extra steps after reaching the goal. But these steps are not just to close out the run, but they propel us into the next race.

The only difference between a sprint and a marathon is that a marathon consists of more steps, more repetition, and continuing the path we are already on. Pop knew that he had relied on God to get him this far, so he had to stay conditioned to rely on God once again. He understood the assignment. His future was not going to be a sprint, but rather a marathon. He knew that he would have to run through the line. He could not stop because people were laughing at him. He had to run through the line. He could not stop because his face was plastered on every major news network. He had to run through the line. Many pastors told him to quit, but he knew that he had to run through the line. He once told me that it was preaching and ministry that was literally keeping him alive. He said that if he stopped, he would die. If he let up or just ran to the line, it would kill him. Mediocrity would kill his spirit. Settling would kill his spirit. Coasting would kill his spirit. This was his calling and so nothing else would be fulfilling and since he was going to inevitably die one day, he might as well live his life to the fullest with reckless abandon giving each day all that he had. Paul says it like this, "I have fought the good fight, I have finished the race, I have kept the faith." 2 Timothy 4:7.

He died in faith, going the extra mile, doing the extra reps, doing the work, and believing the prophecy. Hebrews states that some of our founding faith leaders, like Moses, Abraham, Noah, and others died in faith. Death was the finish line, but their faith propelled them past it, into eternity.

We prayed together, worked out together, walked together, played video games together, took communion together, went to games together, read scripture together and preached together during his final days. We went the extra mile, together. Our last days together were like our first days together, when I was a child and he was just daddy and Reverend Long. We played games together, went to the park, ran together, studied scripture together (the what to do), and more. He could have just laid there while he was suffering and died, but instead, he gave one more rep by being intentional in spending time with my siblings and me, to make another deposit within us, running through the line.

Pop's diligence and faithfulness truly challenged me to remain faithful in my life. Watching a man who had every legitimate excuse to quit, not quit, was one of the best lessons he taught me through demonstration. I can't quit on my family, stop being a son, a father, a friend, a supporter, an encourager, or a minister if the circumstances seem to be unfavorable. Now I get up every day and say to myself, "My dad got up, so I gotta get up." It's oxymoronic that we had our best days together, during his worst days. It hurts my heart that many of these experiences didn't take place until that time, but I'm so grateful, nonetheless, they happened. I don't know if this lesson would have resonated the same if the circumstances were better. It's easier to be strong when you are at full capacity. But when you're not strong, we take joy in The Lord and there we find strength. Some things still sadden me, yet I know that God is joyful and strengthens me to continue on. When I don't feel hopeful, I think about my dad, and continue to hope. When I don't want to be faithful, I think about my dad transitioning, while still believing, and as a result, my faith is restored. When I don't feel loved, I think about my dad, and I continue loving others.

REFLECT NOW...

1. Is your family training together as a team, or individually (in silos)?

2. Do you allow each other to see your strengths and weaknesses?

3. Do you support each other in your areas of growth?

   a. If so, how?

   b. If not, why not? How can you start?

4. What activities excite you to live?

The Call

In the book of Samuel, I believe it's Samuel 3, Samuel as a young man, receives a call to minister the gospel, to be a prophet to nations, and to be the voice of God. Samuel, the one who selected David to be the forthcoming King of Israel, rebuked kings. Samuel was the one who rebuked the people for wanting Saul as their king when they had a legitimate prophet in him and could have been governed by the covenants in the Torah. Samuel was the one who was mentored and apprenticed by the preceding prophet Eli. Samuel, the one who God chose to speak to and through, once Eli had disqualified himself through disobedience. God spoke to Samuel as it is recorded in this text.

Samuel was a little boy and was living in the house of Eli, who was a grown man. Being mentored by Eli, he had become accustomed to his voice, and here it is in the middle of the night when Samuel hears what seems to be the voice of Eli, call him. Once, twice, and thrice, every time Samuel heard his name being called, he would get up and go to Eli and say, "Yes sir, you called me, what do you need?" It took a moment for Eli to figure out having told Samuel each time that he did not call him, but knowing the obedience Samuel had, he recognized that someone must be calling Samuel and if it was not him, it must be God.

Eli had not heard God's voice in so long, he may have even forgotten what it was to hear his voice and how he was to respond. He gives Samuel clear instructions and says, the next time you hear this voice call, simply say, "Speak Lord, your servant hears." As the story goes, God speaks again to Samuel and this time he is obedient to the words of Eli and says, "Speak Lord, your servant hears." Samuel is regarded as one of the greatest prophets, because not only did he hear God, but he also responded consistently in obedience to the directions coming from God.

As ministers of the gospel, we all have gotten into ministry as a response to a call. Many ministers have gotten into ministry because they have literally heard the voice of God speak to them and tell them their purpose within the kingdom. There are others who are being apprenticed or being mentored by a pastor, bishop, reverend, or church leader, who has spoken ministry into them, prophesied it, and called them to the ministry according to their own spiritual acumen.

I hate to say it, but I have to, especially in our present times, there are many who see the glitz and glamour, and think of pastoring as access to cars, service, the power to influence, houses, jewelry, or regalia. But I want to caution anyone reading this. In my opinion, that is not the best way to enter this type of service. Jesus cautions us by saying, woe to those that preach the gospel and ministering for you are responsible not just for lives, but you're responsible for spirits and souls. Doctors and nurses are responsible for lives through their occupations, but a minister is responsible for both our humanity, our growth indignation, and our understanding of our divinity. A mortician is only responsible for the physical body, but as a minister, we're responsible and have a duty to minister to the immaterial portion of our being. We are responsible for catering to bloodlines to break generational curses, shifting paradigms, calling out familiar unrighteousness, raising up leaders, and calling people into everything that God would have them to be.

To this point, true succession and the mantle being passed from one leader to the next, like Elijah to Elisha, is so important, especially in the local church, because it is a kingdom orchestration where families are connected to a leader. Through proper succession, the new leader comes in already knowing the families and the generation that they're merging with because he or she has already established a relationship with those families.

Joshua came from the tutelage of Moses and lived with the people. The same people that Moses was upset with, and was able to lead, he came from amongst them and did life with them. Even the disciples were well received because they could trace their spiritual heritage directly back to Jesus, having worked with him. Not only were they touched by Jesus or had met with him in passing, but they actually had done life with Jesus and Jesus himself anointed them for that specific purpose. They were filled with the Holy Spirit to spread His gospel. It was a transition, and they were called. Joshua and Caleb were called. The disciples were called. Samuel was called. David was called. It's not to say that others could not have potentially fulfilled those roles and done some great work, but would it have been a proper, spiritual, and anointed transfer?

Here it is December 24, 2012, I'm minding my business and in the Christmas spirit, having spent the week celebrating and enjoying various activities; at church with the youth who I was pastoring at New Birth, doing things with my friends, and just going about my normal holiday regimen. I pulled up at Stonecrest Mall to buy some last-minute gifts, trying to catch a sale (something else I learned from my dad). Growing up Pop never bought us gifts in advance. He would wait until an hour or two before the stores were closing because he knew the prices would be slashed. He picked up this habit during a time where his life was much simpler, but he carried this same habit over to the times where money was not as much of a concern.

I arrived at Stonecrest Mall and parked outside of Dillard's department store and had barely gotten out of the car when I received a call from my dad which is nothing strange, but what he said was. He asked me where I was, and I told him I was at the mall. He said, "Alright, well you probably need to hurry and do whatever you have to do there because you are going to be preaching in the morning." I stopped for a moment and said, "What do you mean?" He said, "Well, we're going to start doing a Christmas Day service and you're going to be speaking at it." I said, "Oh really?" with a little laugh and chuckle in my voice. He said, "Yeah, so you need to do what you have to do so you can go ahead and prepare." I said, "Wow, that's the second time you have done that to me, but it's cool, I'm ready."

The first time he did that was back in March of 2009. He called me on an upcoming Monday and told me that he wanted me to speak during bible study on that Wednesday. Now my guy, Pastor Tommy Powell aka Peezy, along with then Elder Darius Wise, had both shared with me their experiences when my dad called them a day or hours before the time he wanted them to minister. Telling them they were going to be ministering, it's so funny because he had no regard for what their previous plans were.

So, when he called me this second time, I realized their words were true and a part of the way Pop mentored us as ministers and preachers. This method included calling us, catching us off guard with an assignment to minister the gospel. Now I want you to understand why this is key. There are many parables, stories, and texts in the *Bible* where leaders had to respond to unexpected things. Leaders had to step up when others were out of pocket or unavailable. Leaders had to always be in tune with what was going on with the people, in world systems, financially, in the community, and on all levels because at any moment, something could take place and leaders had to be able to respond.

Often my friends wondered, "Man, how can it be that you can get a call to be somewhere, and I will be with you the whole time wondering how you're going to pull it off and I see you get up and preach a full message on something?" I shared with them that I had to give the credit to my dad because he trained us in a way that we were always going to be ready. So, my call to ministry didn't come just by hearing from God. My call to ministry came by my dad literally picking up the phone and dialing my number. My call to preaching literally came by being called, called again, called upon, coached, mentored, and being put in uncomfortable situations. My call to ministry came by my father seeing things in me that I was either running from, had recognized but not giving the necessary attention to, or simply that I was not even aware of.

There's an old saying that Pop often shared, it takes a greater man to make a man great. It's true not just for myself but for many men and women all around this world. A part of Pop's gift was the calling in which he was able to speak into people and call out people's greatness that they didn't know was in them. Some of you may be crying right now as you're reading this portion, just by me making that statement, because you wouldn't be doing what you're doing right now, living like you're living, moving in the things of God, had it not been for him literally calling, calling things out of you, and speaking things into you. I learned to be ready for any moment, at that moment.

He asked me did I have anything flowing in my spirit to speak? I said, "Well, I may have one or two things." Honestly, I was just shooting the crap and he must have picked up on it because he said, "Well I got something for you," and he told me that he wanted me to use Luke 2:7 and preach about how there was no room at the inn for Jesus, as well as the neighborhood not making room for Jesus. The church leaders found ways to box Jesus out and didn't make room for him. Many knew that Jesus was the coming king but felt threatened by him and didn't want to give up their seat or their position in order to put him rightfully where he was supposed to be.

Many knew that Jesus was the Son of God and was called for such a time as this, yet they did not make any room for Him in the inn. So, I'm saying to everyone right now who has felt disenfranchised among your family, friends, church, social organizations, and corporately, you may have been boxed out and may not have been granted space, but our God is a way maker and if you can just hold on until the end, you shall get your crown of glory.

Now what was funny is that I ended up being the set Christmas Day minister, at New Birth, until his transition. It was something that I looked forward to doing and I believe the congregants looked forward to participating as well. Whether I was speaking on Christmas day, a regular Sunday Bible study, my dad never saw me minister in person. Anytime that I ministered, he would be seeing it through Livestream wherever he was or watching a replay on DVD, but he never saw me speak in person, and to be honest, that bothered me. It bothered me because I knew there were others who had spoken there, that he considered 'sons' that he was in the building for, whether they were someone from the house or a guest speaker.

It wasn't until January 11, 2016, that I was speaking at a homegoing for a young lady named Jamila. She was the daughter of Sherry Armotrading and had passed tragically. Sherry is a beautiful soul and reached out and said she wanted me and no one else to do the eulogy for her daughter, as we had grown up together. There it is again, that community tie that I mentioned before. We had done life together. I was honored to do it and speak on her behalf, but I hated it was her eulogy versus her graduation or ordination or something more festive.

I shared the eulogy and the title, it was from Kirk Franklin's lyrics, "*Right before I die, I gotta live.*" I rode that wave for about 15 or 20 minutes. Afterwards, my dad texted me and said, "Before I die I got to live! You did a great job. Proud of you and stop running from your true call!!! You are a preacher! Your voice and spirit will deliver many!!! Everything else is side ministry." You should know that while I was speaking, I saw a silhouette in the back of the room that I, for a split second, thought was him, but it was dark back there and I was keeping my attention on the family. When I received that text, it confirmed immediately to me that he was there, and I had such a feeling of joy and affirmation that my dad was in the room and finally had heard me minister in person. It's so crazy because one would have thought that this type of moment would have been at a big-time event on a Sunday morning or during a major service, possibly even a conference or something, but it was at the funeral with maybe two to three hundred people in the room. While I was trying to help a family deal with death, his presence gave me so much life!

I assumed that he must have still been at the church in the building after receiving that text, so I hurried upstairs and tried to catch him. Pop was good at being in the church and then sliding out. I caught him upstairs in the hallway outside of his executive office area. We talked and laughed for a moment and he said, "Long, you pulled that thing." I made him aware that I had received his text and he said, "Yes, it's true." He went on to yet again make another prophetic statement. He said, "As soon as you give yourself over to preaching and ministering the gospel, all of those other things that you have been chasing and trying to do will come to you."

Now just like Samuel, Jeremiah, and Jesus, the words of a prophet are true whether they're here to see them or not. Many prophets were martyred because they spoke things that did not come true, within a certain time frame, people temporarily marked them as false, but my dad spoke a lot of thing that may not have come in his life, but have come true after his death. It reminds me of Dr. Martin Luther King, Jr., who said, "I may not get there with you, but my eyes have seen the glory." Much, if not all, of what Dr. King saw, we are now walking in or on the cusp of.

For the next 3.5 to 4 years, I stopped my music performances, I wasn't on the radio, and the only television endeavor that I did was serving as a cast member on Oxygen Network's, *Preachers of Atlanta*. It's funny because it was about preachers. So, for that period, all I did was preach the gospel. I had more speaking engagements than I ever had in my entire life and these engagements weren't just local or regional. I was called to Africa to speak on numerous occasions, as well as London. I gave myself over to preaching the gospel. Pop and I ministered together on December 25, 2016, which was the best gift ever. We went from him having never heard me speak, in person, to sitting in the back row of the chapel hearing me speak, to us speaking together during his next to last time standing in the pulpit.

During the interim period, in between Bishop Stephen Davis resigning as the pastor of New Birth, and the board of trustees doing a search and selecting a pastor, I spoke at New Birth about six times. Every time I spoke, I felt more anointing. Every time I spoke, I began to see some of the things that my dad and my grandfather had talked about. My paternal granddaddy used to reach out to my dad and ask him if he would see smoke when he preached, and he would tell him, "Eddie if you ain't see black smoke when you preached, then you ain't preaching." One time, my dad gave a message and a prayer, and PawPaw, which is what we called my grandfather, the late Reverend Floyd Morris Long, II, told my dad that it was very educational. In so many words, that was an insult to what my dad had done or an unfavorable response to his preaching. None the less I was starting to understand the smoke.

During this time of being set in one place, speaking consistently, I saw things that I had never seen before. Then something big happened. I watched my dad lay hands on people for years and people would fall out or go down. It had been prophesied to me, by my uncle Pastor James Long aka Uncle Joe, that my hands would be used for healing, and for the first time while I was speaking, I heard the Lord tell me to do an altar call for women who had been going through physical abuse. There were so many women who came down to the altar. I heard the Lord tell me to call my bonus mother, Elder Vanessa Long, over and to touch hands with her, with the anointing oil, and to lay hands on the ladies who had come forward because these ladies needed strength. Since Pop's transition, ML as I called her, had to tap into different levels of herself and even she awakened to certain things that Pop saw in her that she had run from or was not aware of in herself. Now she had begun to operate in that light. That same power and strength she began to find in herself, the women of the church who were hurting, needed to use to be elevated beyond their circumstances.

Jointly, we begin laying hands on the ladies and I say this as humbly as I can because it was not me, but the Lord working through me, I laid hands on one woman and she instantly went down to the floor. Then I touched another, and she too was slain, that had never happened before. I had preached domestically and internationally, but there was something about being where I was supposed to be and building on the spiritual foundation that was previously set in motion. I ministered at New Birth about four times, standing in Pop's place, during the time he was sick with cancer. I will leave that there.

Fast forward, a selection was made that November. The following January, January eleventh to be exact, I received a call. My man Katt, with Radio One Atlanta, invited me to come to the station and have a meeting concerning programming. My friend Canton Jones was moving on to focus on other things and they wanted to discuss filling in that time slot with my own show. Now many years before, I had the habit of going by the radio station, regularly without rhyme or reason, to get a meeting to pitch my show, and clearly, it had not panned out yet. But at this moment, after dedicating myself to three or four years of preaching, something that I was not pursuing at the moment, pursued me. Radio One called me!

Along with my co-hosts, Bre Singeleton and DJ Dex, we launched *Lit Nights with ED* on Praise 102.5 on January 31, 2019. It is my hope that someone understands when God speaks, He's faithful to His word. When God speaks through true prophets, He's just as faithful to His word. As long as your calling is a God calling, though it may seem like you are losing and giving up some things, trust me it's going to work out for your good, according to Jeremiah 29:11. Even now, there are some other things my dad spoke to me that haven't happened yet, but I have these testimonies of his word coming true and things working out just by being obedient that I can take confidence in. I share these stories with you so that you too can have some stories and testimonies to take confidence in concerning the calling on your life. Many are called, but few are chosen. Pop used to ask the question, "who's chosen?" The ones who pick up the phone…

Hey y'all, Jesus is on the mainline.

Who's Your Daddy?

The church has a culture of fatherhood and sonship which I believe in its origin, is aimed to echo the concept that humanity is connected through family. God starts with the family and works through the family to build nations. So, when a nation is destroyed, it means the family must be reconciled to itself. Growing up, I didn't see my dad a whole lot during my adolescent years, but I knew my dad and I had a good relationship with him. I can't say the same for all my friends, so I have valued the father-son relationship, above any other relationship in my life, but it came with many conflicts.

Both my father and my grandfathers were pillars in the community and their mere presence in the lives of those they served was so impressionable that it caused others to call them daddy or father. Nearly everyone that knew my maternal grandfather in his city, called him Daddy Lewis. He was born in 1919. His grandparents were slaves, and his parents were born on the heels of slavery making them first generation free slaves. They came through tough times having walked from Charleston, South Carolina to metro Charlotte, North Carolina where they took dwelling. Daddy Lewis represents survival being a World War II Veteran and an entrepreneur who started two successful businesses during the height of segregation, integration and Jim Crow eras. These events predate the activism of Dr. Martin Luther King, Jr. I say that for the emerging generations to understand that African descendants weren't always driving luxury cars and there were people who paid a major price to pave a way for us all. I challenge everyone reading this to talk to your senior relatives and overstand some of the challenges that your family overcame. I promise that you will find strength, self-worth and value in this knowledge.

While growing up in North Carolina, we quickly had to become accustomed to sharing our grandfather with the entire community. Then when I came to visit my dad, he went from being my dad for a short stint of time to becoming everyone's dad.

I say this as respectfully as I can and being my father's first biological son, in a normal progression of things, the first biological child would have a time where they would be, in essence, the only child and have that time with their parents. When my older sibling Eric was adopted around the same time I was born, though I am the firstborn, I was never the only child.

While growing up, Eric's friends called my dad, dad and my dad had other mentees that he had been mentoring since before I was born that also called him dad. It seemed as when the ministry got bigger, more and more people called him dad. No one really asked me, "Hey is it cool if I call your dad, dad?" Not that they needed my permission, but in the same breath I wasn't going around calling other people's parents, mom or dad. Even when Les Brown was mentoring me, I never called him dad or anything remotely close to it. Even when my mom was seriously dating someone, I never called them dad. So, this may have been a mix of me being affirmed by my dad and not needing to call someone else dad while at the same time having some sense of pride and respect for my dad, to not call someone else dad. Nevertheless, it just was always weird to me.

If you know anything about the Black church culture, you understand that people always refer to their pastor as dad. In the Catholic church, parishioners often refer to the Priest as father, as a symbol that this person is standing in the place of God, our Father, for you to talk, make confessions, and appeal to them as if you were talking to God. But in the African American church, the relationship is much deeper, much more formal, and at the same time, much more casual. People who I never met were calling my dad, dad. Grown men, even some older than him were referring to him as dad, and it wasn't just a one-way street. Pop had a spiritual father who he referred to as his dad, and it was still something I struggled with.

As I read more of the writings and teachings of Jesus, it became even more convoluted to me, whereas, in the scripture, Matthew 23:9, Jesus gives us clear direction to not to refer to any man as father, because there's only one father. I have engaged in many discussions concerning this 'dad thing' over the years, with people who are anti calling another man dad or spiritual father, whereas others who are pro this belief, stating it's referencing that God has placed someone in your life to direct you and be the voice of reason or the voice of God in your life. The flip side of this is that I've seen abuse of this pseudo position in someone's life, which oftentimes have led to more confusion, hurt, and pain, opposed to clarity and direction for those who attempted to align themselves with this belief.

During my dad's homegoing service on Wednesday, January 25, 2017, I shared remarks that many considered to be the eulogy. My statement "Who the Hell Are They?" went viral and recanted in mainstream media. At the suggestion of others, I decided to market the phrase on apparel and stamp it via my media outlets. That statement was a powerful one that spoke to my father's critics and those who feasted on the many rumors about him. It spoke to ministers who cowardly did it behind the scenes versus embodying the spirit of Paul and gently restoring a brother if they believed that he had fallen short of the glory according to Galatians 6:1, "Brothers and sisters, if someone is overtaken in any wrongdoing, you who are spiritual, restore such a person with a gentle spirit, watching out for yourselves so that you also won't be tempted." All things considered; it wasn't the most impactful remark that I shared in my opinion.

There were two other things that I shared that should have resonated with everyone. The remark that I want to focus on is fatherhood. I made a statement concerning those who were in that arena-styled sanctuary who viewed my dad as a father and that for some, he was the only father that they had ever known. On the contrary, he is my dad and I always had a father. I shared that while I resented sharing him, at that moment, I too was fatherless for the first time in my life. Now, for the first time in my life, I could relate to a fatherless person and empathize with them. In that room were some of the Body of Christ's most impactful leaders, yet none of them would be able to fill the void in my life now. None of them possess what Pop possesses. As a matter of fact, many of them viewed him as their father too. Bishop Dale C. Bronner told me that in Hebrew culture, the last step to full manhood was losing your father. Bishop T. D. Jakes told me you never know how much shade the tree was providing nor how much sunlight it was enduring until it is cut down. During this time of transition, I realized that the era of me having an earthly father was done and, in the time since I came to truly see God as a father, The Father!

If you weren't at the homegoing service, if you did not stream it, or if you don't recall my remarks, but you are reading this book and you viewed my dad as your father and have ever felt offended by me, I apologize to you. My childhood was different, unorthodox, and non-traditional, to say the least. Unconventional situations can often cause us to feel insecure in certain areas. Although I was a very confident adolescent, I must admit that other mentees being around my dad, did cause me to think and feel like I wasn't adequate or enough. I recall how difficult it was for me to give Pop gifts, especially on Father's Day. I'm trying to make him something special, with my little coins, while people who made way more money than me, were buying him things that I couldn't afford. How can a son compete with that? Why should a son have to compete with that? My little gifts could not compare. People gave him jewelry, money, clothes, etc. while I'm working, making minimum wage, and trying to save some money to give something that can compete with their offerings. Over time, I just quit competing and focused on what I could do. In Genesis 4:3, we see that Cain killed Abel because he felt that his gift did not compare to Abel's and the pleasure that it brought God. Cain may not have been giving from the heart. He may have been giving from competition. I did not want to be like Cain, I just wanted to be my father's son. So, I quit competing and just gave my best.

Can you imagine nearly every time you come home for visitation, there are new people hanging around your parents calling them dad, and some are your friends while others are celebrities? Many were adults. Can you imagine what that could do to your esteem, confidence, perception of self, or ego? My mind would go so many places. Who are you? Why are you calling him dad? Where did you come from? You are just here for what you can get? Don't you have any self-pride? What do you want? Does this mean that I must accept you as a sibling? Pop really raised quite a few people. He taught them things, let them utilize his vehicles for things like proms, dates, etc., got them jobs, helped with their bills, helped with their education, was involved in their schooling, and more.

Now, for the most part, I had been a good judge of character and did not have an issue with everyone, though I felt that many were in fellowship with my dad, just for what they could get. There were quite a few genuine people with whom I developed friendships that have lasted to this day. Jesus said, when you have seen the son, you have seen the father. I have always felt that the way someone treats your children says a lot about how they feel about you. There were some people, even to this day, who are crazy about Pop, yet never acknowledged us, his children, outside or in his presence.

This is something that I had to learn how to deal with. Check on your pastor or leader's family. Don't assume they're okay and have it all together. They may be emotionally unstable but know how to hold it together in public. They may be one play away from losing it all. They may be more stressed out than you. Check on them. You may be getting more of what belongs to them and what they truly need than they are. It really bothered me when others had experiences with my dad that I did not have. I got to a good place concerning these things when I realized I held a position still that they didn't have, and that is I am his son. That is something that couldn't be taken away, only my siblings and I could own that.

To be honest with you, I never held much compassion for folks when they were calling my dad, dad because it always felt that someone was trying to take something away from me or take a piece of what was mine versus going and seeking out what was theirs. My thoughts were, 'Hey, you didn't get here by yourself. It took two to tango, so you have a father somewhere. Let's potentially focus on honoring your father, whether he's present or not, deadbeat or not, and viewing my dad less as a father and more of a mentor.'

My dad knew that I struggled with this, yet at the same time, he genuinely felt in his heart that a part of his calling in life was to stand in the gap for those who were fatherless and support them as such, I would be remiss if I didn't say it, this purpose also served him. Many of us in life are unfulfilled because we have not identified and/or begun to live in our purpose. Once we live in our purpose, not only is the world a better place, as God's kingdom is being served by us being rightly aligned, but we then also find a different level of happiness, contentment, and comfort, coupled with being rewarded by operating in our purpose.

I like how Bishop Dale C. Bronner states it. He says, "there are three levels to happiness. The first is physical, which is short-lived. The second is passion and the third is purpose. By walking in purpose, we reach the highest and most sustainable level of happiness." Mentoring and fathering others really did make Pop happy. Within our household, he adopted two children, birthed me from his first marriage and my brother Jared from his second marriage and he also parented a foster child. Not to mention, all of those who he closely mentored. Fathering was indicative of who he really was and what he enjoyed doing.

At the same time, from my position, one can begin to wonder if they are enough. Almost like, but not to the degree that of when a wife is married and a husband is still cheating and has two, three, or four side chicks. She may begin to wonder what it is that she is not doing right. Is she inadequate? Now I want to reiterate that what I'm saying is not to that degree, but that's just to give you an example of what I felt from time to time. My siblings may feel different but all four of us have different backgrounds and a different connection with our father! You may even argue with my thoughts, but I say this as honestly and jokingly as I can, this story is not about you, it's about me and my truths.

You know it wasn't until my dad passed away that I could actually empathize and sympathize with the need so many had to call him father. It gave them a sense of belonging and connectedness. If you go back and watch the tape of my remarks from my dad's homegoing, I asked then and I am asking now, for forgiveness concerning my disposition toward the fatherless. Finally, I understood for many, had it not been for my father's voice in their life, they would literally have not made it to where they are.

I came to the understanding that all of this is a part of my purpose. My father has always been a mentor and a fatherly figure to many. My conception, my birth, and now my presence, legitimized him as a biological father and put him on a track to being a good man because God starts with family and builds nations from family. The word of the Lord in Proverbs 13:22 states, "A good man leaves an inheritance to his children's children." As a mentor, coach, and father figure to many, there is a spiritual heritage that's there by us being joint heirs with Christ, but there's no biological heritage. A part of my purpose is to have children. I am called to not only maintain what has been established but also to take it to another level and ensure that things are transferred to the third and fourth generations, thus solidifying that Eddie Long was a good man.

Around 2014, when he and I were having a deep discussion, he shared with me that mentoring those who were in need literally gave him life and gave him joy. It was something about the way he said it to me and the clarity in which he spoke, coupled with me having the ear to hear that I began to accept that this was just who he was and what he loved to do. I came to find out that my dad was aware of my feelings. As I grew older, I realized that Pop was purposefully stretched, overextended, and burdened.

My dad possessed the ability to sense one's emotional state or mindset. It wasn't strange for someone to be in a bad emotional space, yet masking it well, and the issues be felt by Pop. I guess that he sensed I was struggling with my place in his life. In 2001, Pop presented this letter to me as a gift:

Dear EDward 'Kodi' Long,

I was having a hard time trying to figure out what to give you for Christmas. It is very easy to go out and buy you something. As a matter of fact, I buy many people things. If you haven't noticed over the years, I am a giver. I have many people who call me dad, and I have blessed them with all kinds of stuff. I can imagine that at times, when you watch me give things away, to so many young men who call me dad, if you have a special place in my heart. I guess you have days that you feel like you're just like everyone else and sometimes less.

Well, I want to set the record straight. You are my number one son. I am so proud of you and how you have matured. The way you go ahead and handle business, to this day, blows my mind. You are truly a man, and a son after my own heart. This is why I wanted to sit down and write this letter. I wanted to give you what money could not buy, and that is my heart.

I know there are still things I must teach you. I must give you more of my time and communication. I will do better on that. I can also feel your struggle right now, as you're trying to find out your own destiny. Being in school studying one thing, and you got something else in your spirit, is a real pain. I also hear a cry in your spirit, 'does anybody really care about me or just what he or she can get from me?'

Well, son, I really care, and I love you. I'm here for you, and if you ever need me to come to your school, just to be with you for a day, just call me. I will change my schedule because you are that important to me. Now, remember that every great man struggled with their destiny before they walked in it. What separates the man from the boys is true men keep pushing after every disappointment, they fall but they get up. Life is nothing but choices. If you make the right ones you win, and with the wrong ones you learn new things about God, you, and the world.

So, in the words of basketball great, Bill Russell, the game is scheduled, I must play it, therefore I might as well win. My wonderful son life is scheduled today, we must live it therefore let's go ahead and win.

I love you with all my heart. You are my number one son.

Signed,

Eddie L. Long

Since my dad's transition, I have had a few questions about some things, but any time I begin to wonder, I just refer to the letter, because that's the word that my father gave to me and that right there was the measure of accountability. I could hold him to it. I could take confidence in it. I had to learn to let him be him and do the things in life that brought him joy, while at the same time, he had to identify what it was that I needed to have confidence in our relationship.

There's a need for us all to find this same balance in the relationships that we're in, where husbands and spouses can give one another affirmation on where they stand in the relationship while supporting each other in doing the things which bring them personal joy and gratification. This has to also align with their pleasurable and passionate purpose in life.

He was a natural giver. He enjoyed blessing others. He desired to be to us, his biological and adopted children, what his father wasn't to him. Pop often told the story from the pulpit of what was probably his most impactful and liberating conversation that he had with his father, Revered Floyd Morris Long, II. I recall visiting the hospital to see my grandfather who we affectionately referred to as PawPaw with my dad in 1994. A few years before PawPaw had endured a stroke. At this point, his symptoms were becoming terminal. The room that we entered was dark. There were other patients in the room. Pop had me sit in a chair near the front of the room after greeting PawPaw while they talked.

At the time, I was about twelve years old and understood they were having a "grown folks" conversation. This took place, at the end of the era when children were seen and not heard. When Pop would recant this discussion while preaching, he would mention that from birth until this moment, he and my uncles were scared straight of my grandfather. PawPaw was a tall, strong man with a stern demeanor. He grew up in the rural, confederate, Jim Crow south. He ventured to be both a businessman, owning two service stations, where my dad and uncles were employed, while also serving as a pastor, apostle, and evangelist. He moved around to a myriad of churches from Charlotte, North Carolina to Nashville, Tennessee, and Mount Claire, New Jersey. Who knows, maybe this is where Pop developed his apostolic nature. PawPaw was also known for not holding his tongue or fist. I say all of this to support the fact that Pop was very fearful of PawPaw.

For the first time, while PawPaw was disabled in the hospital, Pop finally had the courage to have a long, overdue conversation with his father. Pop asked PawPaw why he never came to any of his football games, why he did not attend his graduation, and why he had never told him that he loved him.

Sitting in a wheelchair, uncertain of his future, with a trembling voice and tearful eyes, PawPaw responded to Pop stating that he, "kept a roof over their heads, food on the table, and clothes on their back." For PawPaw, that was more than his father had done for him. PawPaw didn't have a childhood, as he took on the responsibility of raising himself and his siblings, at an early age in the absence of his father. At this point in time, Pop had been a pastor for many years and was now a consecrated Bishop, yet he still had a fatherhood void in his life. This answer didn't change the past but provided clarity and resolve to a difficult and unaffirmed childhood.

The pendulum swings far to the left and the right before settling in the middle. Almost to the extent that he relished in the responsibility of being a great father to his own children, he also felt the responsibility and burden of being a surrogate father for the fatherless. Pop simply didn't want anyone to feel like he felt growing up. Pop was a momma's boy, who felt abandoned by his father, yet he truly believed that his life's calling was to be a father to many and stand in the gap, as a father, to a fatherless generation. My personal philosophy never bought into the spiritual father concept. Jesus himself instructed us in the book of Matthew to "refer to no man as (spiritual) father for God alone is father." If God is spirit, then God is our spiritual father. That has always been my conviction. It often tickled me that some who considered my dad to be their spiritual father disassociated themselves from him, as he faced trials in the court of public opinion and connected with other leaders as their spiritual father. As my dad's biological son, he will always be my father and I will also be his son. We could have become estranged, separated, mad at each other, or worse, yet there is nothing that we can do to undo or rewrite our biological connection. He is forever my father and I am forever his son.

According to Matthew 18:18, "What is loosed in Heaven is loosed in earth, and what is bound in Heaven is bound in earth." This means that spiritual and natural laws are parallel. Pop and I are timelessly bound in earth and eternally bound in heaven. If one then views a person as their spiritual father on earth, how then can they refute that same spiritual father on earth and identify another spiritual father in the same realm? I view that as spiritual parental abortion. I must say that the parental charades remind me of a Maury Povich episode of 'Who's the Father,' which is why I named this chapter "Who's Your Daddy?" It's time for the sons and daughters of God, to find their identity in Christ, and show their spiritual fruit in their relational convictions. There is a diagnosis that some may possess entitled 'parental schizophrenia.' This means that a person may venture from one spiritual parent to another when things become complicated, or if they don't get what they desire. I am clear that my dad is my only father, and I won't have another. Others can give me a word from God, but God alone is my spiritual father and that settles it for me.

I enjoyed the fruit of my dad's labor when things were beyond good, and I stood with him by his side when it seemed like the world had turned its back on him without knowing or having an indication of the truth. That is what a true son or daughter does! Although my father's conviction and belief about fatherhood was different from mine, frustrating to me, and led to us having to sacrifice and share our father with many, ultimately, I still respected the fact that he was committed to what he believed. The late Bishop Quincy Carswell, who was my dad's friend and first pastor when he moved to Atlanta, Georgia, once told me that my dad wasn't the best preacher. Pop couldn't 'hoop' like Reverend Jasper Williams, or use voluminous words like Bishop Dale C. Bronner, or sing like Reverend James Cleveland and Bishop Paul S. Morton, Sr. But Bishop Carswell told me that it was his mind that other preachers envied. When people slide into my DM, bump into me when I'm out and about, or see me at church and reminisce about my dad, the number one thing that people say that they miss about Pop is his voice. His distinct, reverberating, 1st tenor meets rapper Ludacris' raspy, uniquely comforting, directional, send demons running, Holy Spirit-filled voice.

No matter whether that person is a pastor, businessman, lay leader, young or old, nearly all of them refer to him as dad. It doesn't matter what city, state, country, or galaxy that these people reside in, they still refer to him as dad. Many were members of the church, while some had never met him and only encountered him through his television broadcast, books or recorded sermons. Yet they still felt a fatherly connection with Pop.

Like me, most felt when my dad died, so did theirs. It's an interesting, eerie, complex, and beautiful connection to articulate and comprehend. Pop's mind, kingdom message, relatability, and voice all worked in perfect harmony with zero dissonance to produce a persona that made him fatherly to many.

For those who truly consider themselves to be spiritual sons or daughters of my dad, please know that I am not trying to convince you otherwise. Bishop Jonathan Alvarado once said to me while I was enrolled in his class at Beulah Heights University that, "A keen mind can hold two conflicting thoughts in tension at the same time while understanding both." In layman's terms, intelligence minus emotion will allow us to understand and respect what we don't agree with. If you are convinced that my dad is your spiritual father, I implore you to continue in that conviction. I actually think it is admirable to hold someone with whom you have no biological connection with, with such high esteem. As I stated before, many consider my dad to be their father and have never even met him. Wow! What an honor to bestow upon someone. It's iconic! You possibly possess an ability that I don't. I know I could only share the indescribable love that I have for dad with only my lineage. For you to be able to have that affection for my dad, gives major credence to who and how impactful and magnanimous his material existence was, and his spirit is. To those who once viewed him as your father, but changed your views over time, although I may not like it or agree, I still love you and understand your plight. All is forgiven.

I am my father's first-born child. Recently I got this revelation that blew my mind and helped me to understand my own development concerning capacity as well as my understanding of Jesus. To be the first of anything means that we can expect there to be more. After the first man, there were more beings; after the first car there were more cars; after the first miracle, there were more miracles. The first or the authentic prototype must develop the maturity and unselfishness of not being the only one and sharing its maker with those to come after. Jesus is the "only begotten" son of God, yet we all are sons and daughters of God. Jesus endured more than we can fathom.

In Hebrews 4:15, it states "You have not a high priest who has not been touched with your infirmaries." As I mentioned earlier, since my dad's transition, I now know what it's like to not have a father, to not be able to call him on Father's Day or his birthday, to not be able to reach out for advice, to have questions around your origin that can't get answered, to not have him around to speak on my behalf or cover me, for my children to not meet their grandfather. I feel you! Yet Jesus also endured some things that none of us have, like being crucified or being picked on by other children when he tried to explain who his father was. I too am continually crucified in the court of public opinion, with and like my dad. I have attempted to date some women only for my associates to tell me that the young ladies thought that I was very attractive but they were concerned that I may be homosexual. I have applied for employment at churches and was told that I was more than qualified, but there was too much baggage that comes along with the Long name. I have had pastoral friends who have desired to book me to speak at their churches but weren't able to because their boards or congregation told them no.

Like Jesus, I have experienced times where I have felt forsaken by my father. To the same extent, some of the greatest and miraculous moments of my life were produced by whose I am! I understand that I am graced to do much of what I do because of whose I am, while also ensuring that I have the personal ability, anointing, calling, endurance, skill, and talent to sustain. Ironically, all of these experiences work together, as the Apostle Paul says, to develop my capacity to grasp and understand my dad being a father to not only me, but to the many who came along before, with, and after me. Jesus had to become an unselfish son, receiving all, enduring all, and giving all to all. That's the trajectory I'm on. We are all joint heirs with Christ Jesus. Since my dad's transition, I see the hashtag #BELLlegacy being used affectionately on social media. This stands for Bishop Eddie Lee Long Legacy. This is a legacy that many are part of and grafted into. This makes my heart proud when I see it. It means that his fatherhood and our sacrifice weren't in vain and that many were positively impacted. It means that we are joint heirs.

The letter that Pop wrote to me was like his discussion with PawPaw. It differed as I didn't have to solicit him with my questions because the revelation of fatherhood led him to consider how I may feel. Although the letter didn't give me what I truly desired nor immediately provided more intentional involvement with my dad, it did provide me with perspective, understanding, and consolation.

Most preachers, pastors, bishops, politicians, and other public figures understand the intangibles that come with being the seed of a person or people with notoriety. Missed time can't be recovered. It can be disheartening to watch your predecessor do things with others that you haven't experienced with them. It may not be a spiritual parent to spiritual child relationship, but it may be a mentor to mentee relationship or student to teacher relationship. Nonetheless, I challenge all of the predecessors to be sensitive to the needs of the ones they are primarily responsible for. Do all that you can to affirm them continually. Jesus himself was affirmed by God twice in the scriptures. Once in Matthew 3:17, "And behold, a voice from heaven said, this is my beloved Son, with whom I am well pleased." And again, in Matthew 17:5, "He was still speaking when behold, a bright cloud overshadowed them, and a voice from the cloud said, "This is my beloved Son, with whom I am well pleased; listen to him." If Jesus, being the son of man, needed multiple affirmations, how much more do we? Also, don't do anything with your admirers that you haven't done or don't intentionally plan to do with your own.

Prior to my dad's transition, while walking into the sanctuary at New Birth on Christmas Day in 2016, about three weeks before he transitioned, Pop said to my brother Jared and me, ultimately "there is no greater joy for a father than walking with his sons." For years, Pop had walked that same path with me, as well as some of the most prolific faith and world leaders, associate ministers, staff members, mentees, and others who were mutually honored to be sharing an experience with him. Many of these persons were only there for themselves, disguised in admiration. All in all, during his next to the last walk down this path, he expressed that he had come to this mutually affirming resolution.

Just as my father wrote me a letter, I suggest that we all write a letter to one another. Write your children a letter, write your spouse a letter, write your parents a letter telling them how you truly feel, what you appreciate about them and what you need from them. Tell them how much you love them, affirming their role in your life and yours in theirs. Mean what you say when you write it. We live in such a digital age, where it's so easy to send a text message or send an email, but to take the time to write a letter is a different level of intimacy, intention, and sacrifice. It yields a greater reward. It will provide more clarity, bring more comfort, and be more valuable to the letter's recipient. You don't have to take my word for it, try it and see.

As we close this chapter, I would like to say to all who have viewed my dad as a father, and to the many who view me as a brother, I'm honored to call you brother and sister in Christ as well. Though I lost a lot of time with my dad because of him responding to the desires of his heart, given to him by God, coupled with the purpose and calling on his life to respond to those in need, I ask that you embrace whatever time you had with him and reflect on whatever lessons you learned from him. That's one of the greatest ways to say thank you to him and show love to our family. With the greater understanding that I now have, you can take comfort in knowing I got your back as well. It's an honor and that's what it means for me to be Son of a Bishop.

REFLECT NOW...PARENTS

1. To parents, where are and with whom are you spending most of your time?

2. Are you affirming your seed? How?

3. Have you taken the time to ask them what they need from you and what they value from you?

4. Are there any unresolved issues from your childhood that you are projecting onto your children?

5. How have you turned your childhood pains into purpose?

REFLECT NOW...ADOLESCENTS

1. Have you shared your feelings concerning attention, time spent, and desires with your parents?

2. Please don't wait until you're 41 years old to have a transparent conversation with your parent(s) like my dad did.

3. Find courage in his story to initiate the necessary conversation.

REFLECT NOW...MENTORS/MENTEES

1. For those who are being mentored, are you challenging your mentor to ensure that they have a work-life balance? Are you allowing them to prioritize their work with you above their Godly responsibilities to their family?

2. Are you enabling them to do these things or are you bringing accountability to them?

3. Mentors, are you being accountable to your family and primary relationships above your mentoring relationships?

   a. Have you established boundaries with your mentees?

Outro

I once heard it said, "the best way to live is to be prepared to die." This is a statement that I share when doing eulogies at homegoing's. It is very difficult to think about death. To consider leaving our families, careers, and earthly service to God is not exciting. Considering how we may die may be even more challenging. We didn't get to choose how we entered time and most of us won't choose how we exit into eternity. What we can influence is what becomes of the ministries, businesses, and legacies that we build. We can have a say in who is and is not a part of them. We can dictate what comes of our possessions. After working hard, diligently, and faithfully, we shouldn't leave our legacy up to chance.

REFLECT NOW...PARENTS

1. Do you have plans for your family?

2. Have you pondered what you want your legacy to be?

3. Have you identified who you desire to succeed in your business, role, and operations?

4. Have you put these plans on paper?

5. Who knows about them?

6. Do you have a written will?

7. Do you have an advance directive?

It really doesn't matter how young or mature we are, nor how much or little we may have, we should let our will be known. Once we are prepared to die, we can fully live an abundant, stress-free, and peaceful life.

I'm honored that you took the time to read a portion of my life with empathy and without judgment. I pray that these transparent illustrations have empowered you, your household, and your relationships. As you go forward in life, remember that no relationship is perfect, but with The Holy Spirit, we can continually be perfected, which will allow our best self to be present in all relationships.

Develop the courage to become the best father, mother, son, daughter, friend, spouse, relative, coworker, confidant, and the likes. Apologize quickly, say I love you often, and mean both. Allow your actions to be aligned with your words. I am continually praying for you as I trust you are doing the same for me.

On a few occasions, I've heard Bishop Dale C. Bronner state, "When we are born, we look like our parents, and when we die we look like our decisions." I'm Atlanta born, ATL bred, peace up A-Town down from my toes to my head, and when I transition, I pray to look like the best of my dad, coupled with all that Elohim destined for me to be.

I close in the words of Bishop Eddie Lee Long by saying, "God You said it, we believe it, that settles it."

#Don'tStopKeepGoing
#BishopEddieLeeLongLegacy
#BELLlegacy
#SonOfABishop

Legacy Building: Look Book

It is my hope that you are encouraged from viewing my look book. You may recognize some folks, others you may not, but know they all had an impact on me! *In photos, with more than one individual, their names appear from left to right.*

The Consecration

Chris 'Ludacris' Bridges

David Gagliardi & Sha'Nod Johnson

The Long Lineage:
Destiny, Jared, Vanessa, Nicole, Serenity,
Eric Gagliardi, & Taylor

Eric Gagliardi Long & Jared Long

Eric Gagliardi Long, Jeremy Gunter, Vanessa Long, & Jared Long

J Moss, Justin 'Lil Rocc' Williams, Tyrese Gibson, & Corey Smith

Son of A Bishop

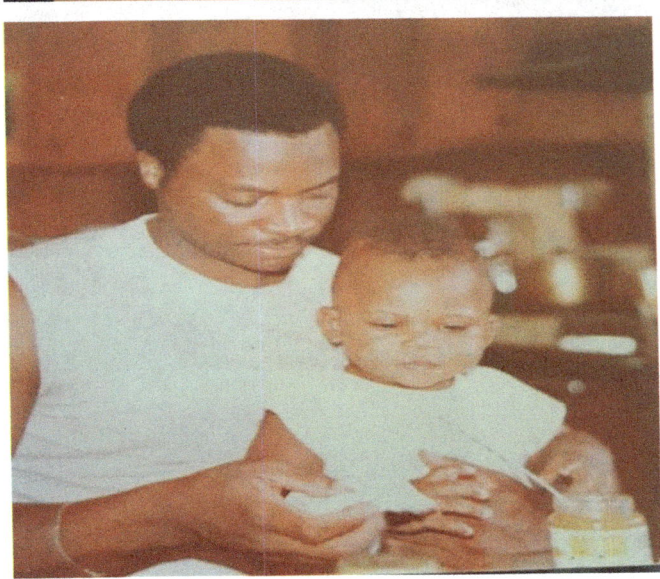

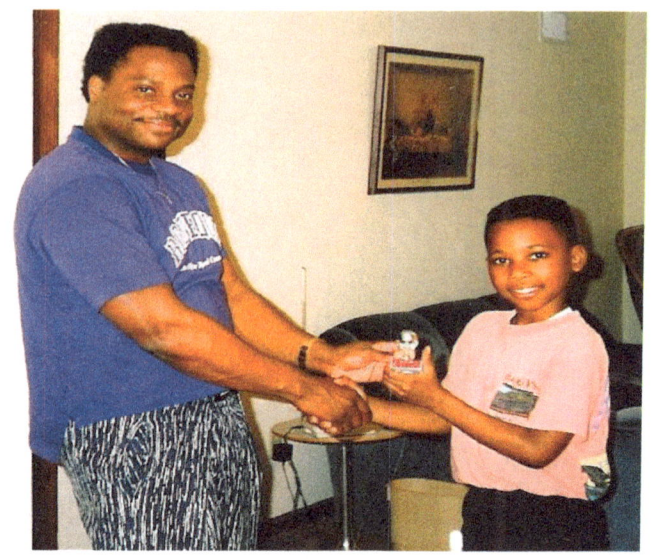

Steve Harvey

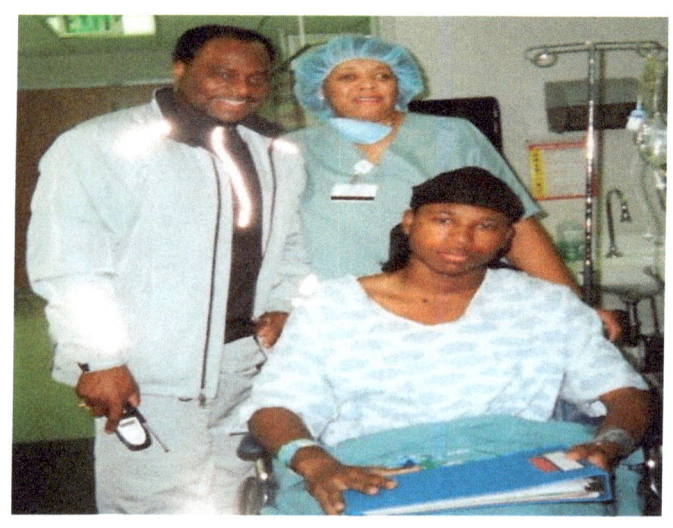

Jared Long

Jared Long & Eric Gagliardi Long

Jared Long & Jeremy Gunter

Jared Long, Taylor Long, Vanessa Long, Monte Campbell, & Rico Love

Louis Farrakhan Jr., & Louis Farrakhan Sr.

Marie Gagliardi, Eric Gagliardi Long, Monte Campbell, Destiny Long, Vanessa Long, Nicole Long, and David Gagliardi

Portia Kirkland

Rico Love & Tiny Lister (aka Debo & Zeus)

Newt Gingrich & Cynthia McKinney

The Longs: Taylor, Vanessa, & Jared

The Longs: Vanessa, Jared, Taylor, & Eric

The Extended Long Family

Like Father, Like Son…

The Legacy Continues!